A Wild Promise

PRINCE WILLIAM SOUND

DEBBIE S. MILLER *Photography by* **HUGH ROSE**

BRAIDED RIVER

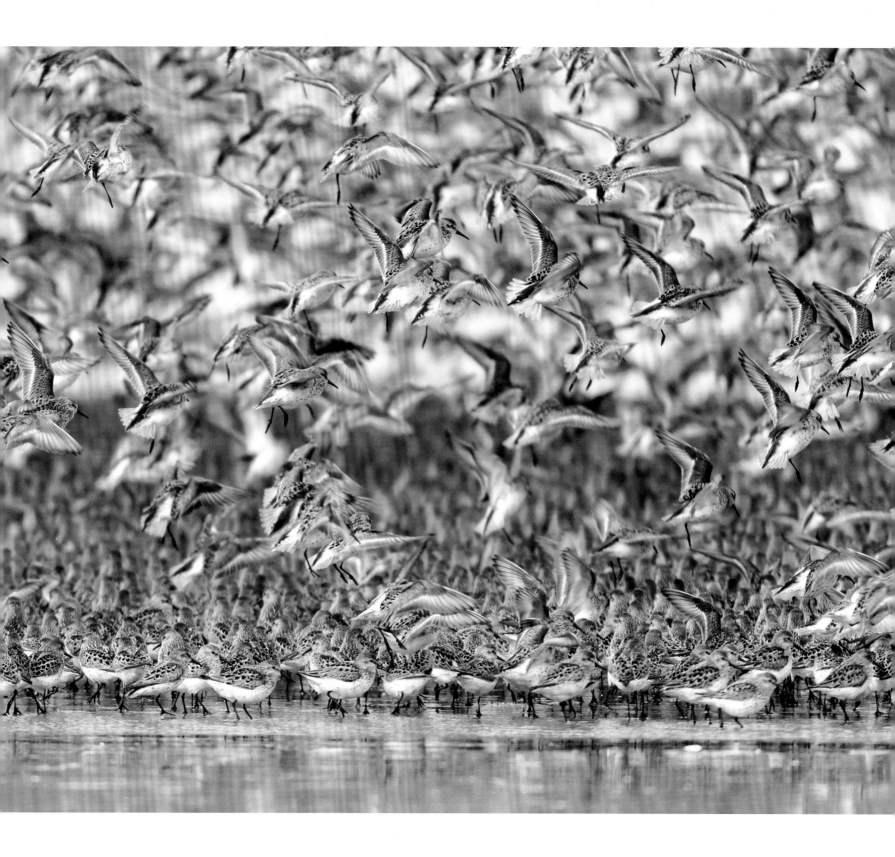

Contents

Map 17

Preface 19

Introduction 23

   Glaciers Bring Life 27

   Journey Up College Fiord 63

   Through the Eyes of John Muir 87

   Islands 101

   Where Is the Columbia Glacier? 123

   The Great Temperate Rainforest 145

   Loss and Hope 159

Epilogue: A Promise of Wilderness 169

Author Acknowledgments 170

Photographer Acknowledgments 171

Bibliography 172

Prince William Sound

THE NELLIE JUAN–COLLEGE FIORD WILDERNESS STUDY AREA

Nestled below the ice-capped peaks of the Chugach Mountains, the Nellie-Juan–College Fiord Wilderness Study Area (WSA) is the beating heart of Prince William Sound. This vast wilderness, with its bays, coves, fjords, rainforests, and glaciers is hard to fathom and the facts barely begin to tell its story. In short, the WSA is

- the largest Forest Service wilderness study area in the United States, established by Congress under the 1980 Alaska National Interest Lands Conservation Act;

- 2.1 million acres, the size of Yellowstone National Park;

- part of the 5.6-million-acre Chugach National Forest, the third largest national forest in the United States;

- surrounded by Prince William Sound, which is about the size of Puget Sound in Washington State and is roughly seventy miles across;

- on the northern edge of the largest temperate rainforest in the world, which stretches from Alaska to the redwood forests of Northern California;

- home to the largest concentration of tidewater glaciers in America—twenty-one glaciers that flow down to the waters of Prince William Sound through a dozen major fjords;

- part of the wildest and most roadless National Forest in the United States, with access mostly by boat from Whittier and Valdez;

- home to many terrestrial and aquatic mammals including black bear, mountain goat, Sitka black-tailed deer, wolverine, marten, mink, river otter, sea otter, Steller sea lion, harbor seal, Dall's porpoise, orca, and humpback whale;

- the traditional homeland of the Chugachmiut people, who have lived around Prince William Sound for at least forty-five hundred years;

- the last bastion for the yellow cedar (*Chamaecyparis nootkatensis*), an elegant rainforest tree threatened by climate change;

- home to four species of Pacific salmon that spawn in approximately two thousand streams around the Sound;

- home to a vast diversity of waterfowl, such as puffins, common loons, arctic terns, pigeon guillemots, kittiwakes, murres, cormorants, auklets, tundra swans, harlequin ducks, and marbled and Kittlitz's murrelets;

- a forest sanctuary for nesting songbirds, such as the hermit thrush, Steller's jay, song sparrow, chestnut-backed chickadee, yellow and Wilson's warblers, and varied and Swainson's thrushes;

- home to the Nellie Juan River, a proposed addition to the National Wild and Scenic Rivers System, a wildlife corridor for brown bears, moose, and wolves;

- the place where, in 1964, the largest recorded earthquake in North America thrust islands up in Prince William Sound by as much as forty feet and brought devastation through a massive tsunami;

- just west of Bligh Reef, where in 1989 the *Exxon Valdez* oil tanker spilled more than eleven million gallons of crude oil into the pristine waters of the Sound, killing countless animals.

The use of "fiord" for College, Harriman, and Nassau fiords is in accordance with the official spelling by the US Board on Geographic Names. Otherwise throughout the book, the more commonly accepted spelling "fjord" has been used.

The map does not show boundaries for state, Native Corporation, and other privately held land within and adjacent to the Chugach National Forest.

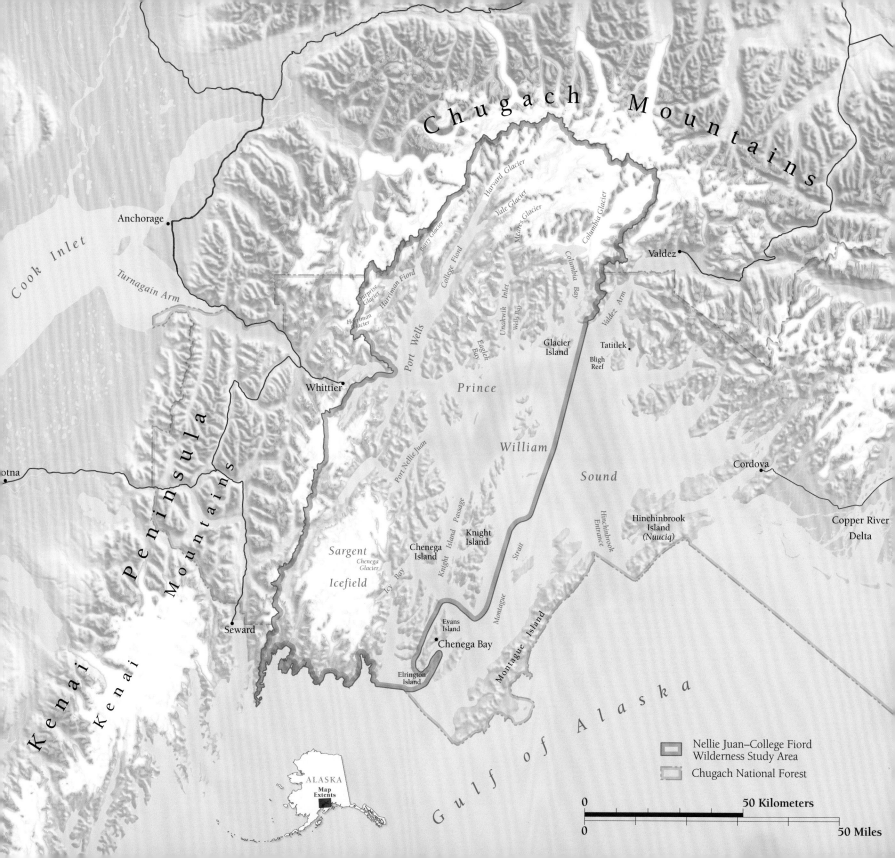

Chugach Mountains

Cook Inlet

Anchorage

Turnagain Arm

Kenai Peninsula Mountains

Kenai Peninsula

Kenai

otna

Seward

Whittier

Surprise Glacier

Harriman Glacier

Harriman Fiord

Port Wells

Port Nellie Juan

Sargent Icefield

Chenega Glacier

Icy Bay

Chenega Island

Knight Island Passage

Knight Island

Evans Island

Elrington Island

Chenega Bay

Barry Glacier

College Fiord

Harvard Glacier

Yale Glacier

Mears Glacier

Columbia Glacier

Columbia Bay

Unakwik Inlet

Wells Bay

Esther Island

Eaglek Bay

Prince

William

Sound

Glacier Island

Bligh Reef

Valdez

Valdez Arm

Tatitlek

Cordova

Copper River Delta

Knight Island Strait

Montague Strait

Montague Island

Hinchinbrook Entrance

Hinchinbrook Island (Nuuciq)

Gulf of Alaska

ALASKA
Map Extents

Nellie Juan–College Fiord
Wilderness Study Area

Chugach National Forest

0   50 Kilometers

0   50 Miles

Preface

"We need a book. But first you need to see this place," said Debbie Miller. So began my conversation with her and Hugh Rose in a bar in Fairbanks on my first day back to civilization after an all-too-brief rafting trip in the Arctic National Wildlife Refuge. Debbie, Hugh, and I had collaborated before. Through numerous past publishing and outreach efforts we had worked to prevent oil drilling in America's Arctic. This time our discussions revolved around 2.1 million acres of the Chugach National Forest in southern Alaska, a wilderness study area established by the 1980 Alaska National Interest Lands Conservation Act (ANILCA), the largest lands conservation act in US history. The fate of this wilderness study area was expected to be resolved in a few years, yet it is still in limbo decades later.

Even before ANILCA, locally and nationally, many citizens had long supported wilderness protection in western Prince William Sound, and this effort has been sustained over generations. Voices for wilderness include commercial and sport fishers who rely on healthy fisheries, subsistence and sport hunters and guides who rely on abundant wildlife, and business owners who cater to outdoor recreation and tourism. Local residents and families rely on the region's wealth of wild foods, including berries, mushrooms, and fish. Ancient rainforests keep carbon out of the atmosphere and serve as magical places to bring friends, raise a family, and expose children to the magic and wonders of the natural world.

The path toward wilderness designation and protection was complicated by the horrific disaster on March 24, 1989, when the *Exxon Valdez* careened off course, split open, and spilled eleven million gallons of crude oil into the pristine waters of Prince William Sound—killing thousands of mammals and seabirds and coating and spoiling untold miles of land and sea.

The disaster and subsequent cleanup efforts compromised the wilderness character of the area.

The public response has been clear and consistent: protect this area by designating it as wilderness. What will this take? Literally an act of Congress.

Debbie, Hugh, and I determined that we would do what we could to tell the story of this extraordinary place and to support grassroots efforts to achieve the wilderness designation crucial to its preservation. One week later, I was aboard the *Discovery*, a sixty-five-foot vessel built in the 1950s, nimbly making its way amid the astonishing splendor of massive glaciers and deeply forested islands of Prince William Sound's interior passages. This was my introduction to the Nellie Juan–College Fiord Wilderness Study Area.

As is so often the case with dwindling wild public land, the Nellie Juan—located along the western edge of Prince William Sound—is remote, achingly pristine, largely unheard of, and in the crosshairs of those who rather bloodlessly refer to "resource extraction potential." In other words, it is a target for short-term exploitation and ruin. Our mission on this voyage was to discuss how we could express the magnificence all around us and how a book could play a role in engaging the region's inhabitants and all Americans. Could we inspire deep discussions about the fate of this public land and the fate of our own human communities in the region? Through a book we would strive to bring the Nellie Juan into sharper focus.

I believed that Hugh's sensitive and in-depth catalog of images would convey the abundance of life, the timelessness of seasons, and vastness of land. And I was confident that Debbie would translate her rich experiences exploring these remote landscapes into vivid, engaging prose. What I was not prepared for was a lesson from Dean Rand, captain of the *Discovery*, and his importance to the telling of this story.

OPPOSITE—*The two tributaries of Radcliffe Glacier feed into Harvard Glacier, the second largest glacier in Prince William Sound, before it empties into the northern end of College Fiord.*

FOLLOWING PAGE—*A black oystercatcher searches for food in fucus beds at the entrance to Copper Bay on Knight Island.*

Dean epitomized not only time-earned knowledge of the life and land of Prince William Sound but also wisdom. His resolve, tenacity, and love of place were almost tangible. He was worried about what might happen if people were not aware of what was at stake and did not weigh in, and he saw that this landscape in limbo could flip from wild to domesticated—and damaged—with the stroke of a pen. As I sat in his compact wheelhouse, we talked while he guided us to glaciers, islands, bays, coves, and deep fjords lined with rookeries, where we would see splendid mountains, wildflowers, and waterfalls and meet oyster farmers and commercial fishers. And the word *displaced* came to mind. If development ran rampant and unchecked, it was not only whales, puffins, salmon, bears, and sea otters who would struggle—it was also Dean and his family and human community who would become unmoored, without ground, homeless.

Dean was wholly committed and made me believe that one person can make a difference. Through his own initiative, he was making connections and opening up opportunities for political engagement, for himself and for others. Grassroots activism at its best. This region was once encased in ice, and it has responded to the ever-changing whims that alter the natural cycles of life over and over again. This is a place too precious to exploit. If we can leave this wilderness area as is, it will serve as a source of wonder, solace, food, and community for future generations of Alaskans and for visitors from around the globe. Sharing this special place shapes our lives, but it also unites us.

I hope that we have successfully conveyed a sense of the Nellie Juan–College Fiord Wilderness Study Area. I hope too that we have shown how important it is for people—for humanity—to be connected strongly to wild rhythms and to a special wild place.

Get in touch. We will let you know how you can make a difference.

—*Helen Cherullo, Publisher, Braided River*

A single kayaker is dwarfed by calving ice, Meares Glacier.

Introduction

When John Muir explored Alaska's coast as a member of the 1899 Harriman Expedition, he was awestruck and captivated by the grandeur of Prince William Sound. The *George W. Elder* steamed along majestic fjords beneath some of the highest coastal mountains in the world. To Muir, a passionate lover of glaciers, this landscape embraced the richest and most intricate range of glacial sculpture he had ever seen.

Imagine what it must have felt like for Muir, on his seventh and final voyage to Alaska. This brilliant, humble man, who first proposed that a massive river of ice carved Yosemite Valley, suddenly found himself among the largest concentration of tidewater glaciers in North America. His detailed sketches and field notes are a testament and a tribute to the wonders of this spectacular wilderness.

When I first saw Prince William Sound and the surrounding Chugach and Kenai mountains, I was on an airplane descending toward Anchorage. The extraordinary view captured me. It was hard to believe that such a magnificent, roadless wilderness, with endless ridges of snowy peaks, countless glaciers fingering toward the water, and lush forested slopes, could be just an hour's drive from the city. I was eager to explore those remote fjords, camp on quiet coves, and write about this enticing place where land and sea are woven together.

That dream became reality over the past five years, thanks to the generous guidance and support of Tim and Barbara Lydon, wilderness stewards for the Chugach National Forest, Dean Rand of Discovery Voyages, and photographer and naturalist Hugh Rose. Their love for the wilderness that surrounds the Sound, and their commitment to protect it, became the driving force for the creation of this book.

Prince William Sound is the shimmering geographic heart of the Chugach National Forest, America's third largest national forest. Like circulating blood, tidal currents ebb and surge through the many fjords and inlets that feed the Sound. This is a major mixing zone, where ocean currents stream in from the Gulf of Alaska and blend with glacial meltwater that flushes out of the fjords. Such an interchange of freshwater, saltwater, minerals, and organic material supports a swirling gyre of life. The Sound is really a giant estuary protected from the rough waters of the Pacific by the islands that encircle it.

Where else in the world can you observe humpback whales breaching, harbor seals giving birth on ice floes, bears snatching salmon, kittiwakes and puffins nesting on cliffs, hermit thrushes singing in a lush rainforest, sea lions basking on the shore, and immense pinnacles of glacial ice thundering into the sea—all on the same day?

Theodore Roosevelt recognized the exceptional nature of North America's temperate rainforest, a lush and vast stand of trees that hugs the Pacific coast from Alaska to Northern California—the largest temperate rainforest in the world. The northern portion of that rainforest fringes Prince William Sound and is part of a dramatic world of tidewater glaciers and mountains that rise thousands of feet above the sea. With the stroke of a pen, President Roosevelt established Alaska's Chugach and Tongass national forests in 1907, the greatest swath of coastal forest in Roosevelt's conservation legacy.

Beyond the trees, the Chugach National Forest is a place where you can witness glaciers carving and grinding the mountains, where new land is born as glaciers melt and retreat in the face of a warming climate. It is a place where you can experience the evolution of a landscape in real time.

The growth patterns of the rainforest reflect this dynamic world. In one moment, you might touch a hemlock that took hundreds of years for its three-inch-diameter trunk to grow on a mountain slope buried in snow most of the year. Next you might gaze at a giant

OPPOSITE—Aerial view of Cascade, Barry, and Coxe glaciers in Barry Arm. During the 1899 Harriman Expedition, the upper part of Barry Arm was locked in glacial ice.

Sitka spruce near the shore, regal and moss-cloaked, where a pair of endangered marbled murrelets might be nesting in the canopy. Then you might spot a young, tenacious alder rooting into a rocky moraine that was recently deposited by the massive plow of a glacier.

The Chugach National Forest is a time travel forest. Its slow-growing trees have adapted to harsh winters, heavy snow, rocky soils, and geologic forces that include glaciation, tectonic shifts, and earthquakes. You can paddle by a ghost forest of skeletal trees and be reminded that the epicenter of the largest recorded earthquake in North America occurred here in 1964.

The human history of Prince William Sound spans millennia, from the indigenous Chugachmiut people, who have lived here for at least forty-five hundred years, to the Russian, English, and Spanish explorers who sailed into these waters in the mid-eighteenth century, the sea otter fur traders of the late eighteenth century, and the gold seekers, copper miners, fox farmers, and commercial and subsistence fishers from the nineteenth and twentieth centuries.

Unlike most of our world, the Chugach National Forest is far wilder now than it was one hundred years ago. Gone are the miners, fox farmers, and fish canneries. Subsistence and commercial fishers continue to harvest the abundant salmon and other sea life, such as shrimp, crab, halibut, and black cod. Several hatcheries enhance the salmon runs in Prince William Sound. Yet the land that embraces the Sound remains roadless and unaltered.

In recognition of the extraordinary wilderness values of the Chugach National Forest, Congress designated 2.1 million acres of the 5.6-million-acre forest on the west side of the Sound as the Nellie Juan–College Fiord Wilderness Study Area as part of the 1980 Alaska National Interest Lands Conservation Act (ANILCA). This wilderness area is about the size of Yellowstone National Park and is home to some of Alaska's famed animal species—black bears, salmon, bald eagles, and mountain goats; and in the surrounding waters, orcas, humpback whales, sea lions, harbor seals, and sea otters.

Nearly forty years have now passed since Congress designated this wilderness study area. It is surprising and worrisome that the third largest national forest, one of the wildest and most spectacular in North America, has not one acre of officially designated wilderness. This is a case of unfinished business that was initiated through one of America's greatest conservation acts. Should such a magnificent place still be a "study area" after four decades?

Visitor use in the Chugach wilderness has skyrocketed since the Whittier train tunnel opened to cars in 2001, bringing more boats and people. The US Forest Service faces challenges to manage the wild character of the area, from unauthorized structures and increased hunting pressure to invasive species and camping litter. There are concerns about oil spills and proposed mining. The Sound and all its marine wildlife and its local people continue to heal from the toxic effects of the 1989 *Exxon Valdez* oil spill. If we are not vigilant, one of Alaska's remarkable places, a dynamic coastal wilderness, may gradually erode away, piece by piece.

In the pages that follow, I invite you to join photographer Hugh Rose and me as we journey through the magnificent Nellie Juan–College Fiord Wilderness Study Area. Experience this dazzling place up close as we explore mirror-calm fjords, tidewater glaciers, temperate rainforest, wild islands, empty beaches, quiet coves, alpine meadows, and peat bogs.

Paddle along, and witness the sheer beauty of this wilderness, where creatures live in aquatic and terrestrial worlds with no boundaries. Along the way you'll meet some of the people who live and work on the Sound, and experience the diversity of wildlife. By learning about this magical place and its inhabitants, I hope you fall in love with it, as I have. And I hope you will better understand why it's so crucial to protect this rare gift of land and sea.

OPPOSITE—*A family of orcas with a young calf cruises the coastline hunting fish near the mouth of McClure Bay in Port Nellie Juan.*

Glaciers Bring Life

Where Ice Meets the Sea

Glassy, calm waters and warm temperatures give us a perfect day to explore Port Nellie Juan Fjord. Each of the dozen passengers holds a camera or binoculars with great anticipation. Most of us have never seen the face of a tidewater glacier. It's hard to imagine the power of massive ice walls and the thunderous calving of glaciers.

A seasoned captain, Dean Rand motors the *Discovery*, his beautiful 1950s boat, toward Derickson Bay. Looking up the fjord, I see a thick spruce and hemlock forest spilling from granite mountains to the water's edge. We are surrounded by the snowy, glacier-clad peaks of the Chugach and Kenai ranges. In all directions, waterfalls plummet to the sea, dazzling white ribbons over dark rock. Every mile on the water offers a new and breathtaking view.

In 1887, another captain ventured up this fjord, in his schooner the *Nellie Juan*. While surveying Prince William Sound for its fisheries potential, Samuel Applegate explored and mapped this region. He must have loved his boat, since he named the fjord after her. Applegate did not know that the surrounding magnificent wilderness would one day be part of the Chugach National Forest and that Congress would designate these surroundings as part of the 2.1-million-acre Nellie Juan–College Fiord Wilderness Study Area.

OPPOSITE—*A boat is dwarfed by the massive face of the Nellie Juan Glacier—one of many retreating tidewater glaciers in Prince William Sound.*

With that mouthful of a name, it is better described as the Chugach wilderness, honoring the Chugach Alutiiq people who have lived in the region for thousands of years. Hereafter, I'll refer to the wilderness study area as the Chugach wilderness.

Dean drops a clanking anchor in a sheltered spot in Derickson Bay. We eagerly zip up our life vests. One by one, we step into an inflatable raft (our dinghy) with naturalist guide and photographer Hugh Rose. Both Dean and Hugh have a deep love for Prince William Sound and the surrounding Chugach wilderness. They have explored the area for decades and shared its wonders with people from all over the world.

Ten of us are experiencing our first adventure here, including my friend Lori Chase, a high school teacher from Fairbanks. She and I have lived in Alaska for many years, but neither of us has explored Prince William Sound by boat.

Hugh maneuvers the dinghy through an obstacle course of floating icebergs that sparkle and glow in the early evening light. Each iceberg is unique in size, shape, and color. Bergs with densely compressed ice are an astonishing, otherworldly blue. The denser the ice, the bluer and more surreal. Other glacial fragments are full of air bubbles and colorless. This porous ice speaks to us as it melts. The bubbles pop and crackle as centuries-old air is released. "That's bergie seltzer," Hugh says, describing the fizzling sound in glacier lingo.

It is so calm that we also hear the breathing of harbor seals as they surface and take a quick breath. They curiously stare at us with black liquid eyes, their wet faces glistening. Then they slip quietly below the glazed surface of the bay, as if camera-shy.

As we slowly motor through the gallery of ice sculptures, Hugh spots a group of harlequin ducks in the distance. About fifty of them skitter across the water, unable to fly because they are molting. Not far from these striking, colorful ducks are several oyster-catchers along the shore, probing among the rocks for

mussels and crabs. Their elongated, orange beaks are bright beacons against their ink-black feathers.

As we round a bend in the fjord, Lori's eyes widen, and she claps a hand over her mouth. I'm thinking she must see a bear on shore until I look over my shoulder. The massive white face of the Nellie Juan Glacier looms above us. At the head of the fjord, the dramatic frontal wall of ice rises about two hundred feet above the water. Beyond, we can see the heavily crevassed glacier fisting through the mountains from the immense Sargent Icefield.

Like a river cascading over a terraced bed, the Nellie Juan descends to the sea for several thousand feet in a series of immense ice steps. Given the magnitude of the glacier's dazzling twenty-story-high face, the chiseled mountains that encircle us, and the steel-blue waters full of drifting ice, our raft suddenly feels like a bathtub toy.

Over time, this colossal tongue of ice gouged and scoured an impressive, narrow fjord, leaving polished granite walls that plunge into the water. Hugh, a geologist, explains that the bulldozing force of the glacier swept away loose, softer rock, exposing the beauty of the gray granite in the same way that glaciers created Yosemite Valley. Such glacial power allows us to see the core, strength, and endurance of crystallized granite.

The steep granite walls create fantastic resonance for the voice of this active tidewater glacier. Small hunks of ice sporadically crumble and fall from the glacier's face, making clapping, crinkling, or rumbling sounds amplified by the stone walls. Tidewater glaciers speak in a dynamic language governed by temperatures and the movement of melting ice.

Crack! Some part of the glacier is fracturing, sending forth a gunshot signal of what is to come. A teetering obelisk of ice begins to peel away from the glacier's snout. Everyone gasps. This ice pinnacle leans unexpectedly in slow motion. Suddenly the mass of ice gives way to gravity, and there's a roaring, thunderous

splash and a stupendous *Kaa-BOOM!* Everyone gazes in disbelief.

Concentric waves radiate from the epic splash toward our boat. The upheaval attracts swarms of crying kittiwakes that dive into the upwellings, catching small silvery fish rising to the surface. At a safe distance, we watch thousands of chunks of ice rise and fall, undulating in a graceful dance on the water as the waves ripple toward us.

The voice of this living glacier is just as impressive and unique as the sight of it, from the gunshots, booms, and roars to the subtle drips, trickles, and whispers of bergie seltzer. We are listening to an ice symphony in a granite amphitheater created by the Nellie Juan Glacier.

Mountains Feeding Whales

Later in the day we motor slowly up Nassau Fiord, approaching another rampart of towering ice. With sheer, polished rock cliffs as shoulders, the two-hundred-foot-high face of the Chenega Glacier hems the fjord, a three-mile-wide ice brow. The glacier is heavily crevassed, almost wrinkled-looking from melting and movement. Like the Nellie Juan, this tidewater glacier steps down to the sea from the Sargent Icefield, a massive basin of ice roughly twenty-five hundred feet above sea level. In the distance, we can just see the edge of it.

To imagine the expansiveness of the Sargent Icefield, picture an enormous, deep mountain lake twice the size of Lake Tahoe. Then picture fifty major rivers pouring from that lake, spilling down the mountains in all directions, plummeting to the sea. Freeze that scene in your mind so the enormous lake becomes an ice field and the rivers become glaciers. Like rivers, the glaciers flow but so slowly that they appear motionless. Yet they move with an astonishing force due to

Blue ice shed from the Nellie Juan Glacier drifts in front of a stream cascading over exfoliating granite.

the massive weight of winter snow and ice compressed over thousands of years.

Consider that a cubic foot of ice weighs about fifty-seven pounds, and imagine standing on the surface of a fifteen-hundred-foot-thick glacier. The weight of the square-foot ice column beneath your feet would be eighty-five thousand pounds. Now recall that the ice is slowly moving. The unimaginable grinding force turns bedrock to powder—fine grains of iron, phosphates, and other minerals, known as rock flour. When that rock flour mixes with water, it has a cloudy, almost creamy appearance, often referred to as glacial milk. This turbid, mineral-rich glacial outflow runs into the sea and fosters the growth of phytoplankton, krill, and small fish that are food for seabirds, salmon, harbor seals, and whales.

Tidewater glaciers crush and transport minerals from mountain to sea, infusing oceans with the building blocks of life. Glacial milk nourishes marine animals and is one of the reasons why nearshore waters are so productive next to tidewater glaciers. When a seabird snatches a sand lance, a harbor seal catches a capelin, an angler hooks a salmon, or a whale swallows a cloud of krill, it's the work of tidewater glaciers that helps create this abundance of life.

Who would have thought that the strong bones, blood, and flesh of a humpback whale are made of mountains pulverized by the might of glaciers?

Kittiwake Colony

As we approach the Chenega Glacier, the grandeur of the scene is mesmerizing. On the glacier's face, Nassau-blue seracs and gleaming ice towers teeter toward the water, ready to break away at any moment. There is constant suspense in this unfolding story. If you look away for a moment, you might miss something big.

Humpback whales carry the minerals of mountains in their bodies, thanks to the tidewater glaciers that crush the bedrock and transport it into the sea.

Not far from the boat, we see rock cliffs bursting with black-legged kittiwakes. Countless nests are stacked on top of one another, like apartments in a tall building. While some of these gulls tend their chicks or eggs, others swarm above us calling. They incessantly repeat their name: *kit-ti-wake, kit-ti-wake, kit-ti-wake!*

These birds have precariously constructed nests in death-defying locations, some more than one hundred feet above the water. From a distance it appears that each pair of birds is dangling in a bivouac tent on a sheer rock wall, like climbers on El Capitan. I wonder, how do these birds tend their eggs on such vertical cliffs with no guardrails?

Taking a closer look through binoculars, I see that each precipice offers a small ledge or a crevice so that the birds have just enough space for a nest with one to three eggs. The bowl-shaped nests are a messy weave of grasses and seaweed plastered with guano and mud. There are so many nests that streaks of guano cover most of the cliff walls like white graffiti.

The kittiwake is a graceful flier and the only gull that dives below the sea surface for a meal. Its colony is in close proximity to the calving glacier for a good reason. Ice from this active tidewater glacier frequently crashes into the fjord, stirring the water and churning up fish such as capelin and sand lance. This rich forage is food for a diversity of seabirds, such as arctic terns, Kittlitz's murrelets, pigeon guillemots, and puffins.

The kittiwake colony is one of about two hundred seabird colonies that thrive in the

Black-legged kittiwakes fly over their colony located on a cliff side near Whittier in Passage Canal.

glacial fjords of the Chugach wilderness and on small, largely predator-free islands scattered across Prince William Sound. More broadly, it's staggering to think that approximately fifty million seabirds nest along Alaska's coast each summer in more than eighteen hundred identified colonies. Drawn by lingering daylight, open space, and an abundant food supply, Prince William Sound and the Chugach wilderness offer excellent habitat for well over one hundred species of seabirds, shorebirds, and other water birds.

Many of these species suffered tremendous losses when hundreds of thousands of birds perished in the *Exxon Valdez* oil spill. During the horrific aftermath of the spill, among oiled birds whose carcasses could be identified, ninety-one species were found. It is now going on three decades, and some species have gradually recovered and stabilized. Yet there are still lingering effects from oil in the environment, and other species, such as the pigeon guillemot, marbled murrelet, and black oystercatcher, have not fully recovered.

By the grace of tidal currents, wind, and glacial outpouring, the long fjords of the wilderness study area were largely spared from oil spill damage. Much of this spectacular wilderness is located in the western part of the Sound, out of the spill's reach.

An adult black-legged kittiwake and month-old chick perch on their nest in late summer. Kittiwakes are the only gull-like bird in the world to build cliff dwellings, and instinct guides the chicks to stillness so they don't fall.

A Birthplace for Seals

Moving up the fjord, the *Discovery* enters the iceberg zone that skirts the Chenega Glacier. Dean carefully picks his way through the bergs, avoiding any that might damage the boat. The puzzle pieces of ice come in all shapes and sizes, from enormous slabs and pancake ice floes to creature-like forms and small chunks of ice known as brash. The colossal face of the Chenega Glacier sheds hundreds of icebergs each summer day.

From a distance the glistening ice floes look peppered with rocks and moraine debris, but as we move closer, I'm stunned. The enormity of the glacier has altered the scale of this mosaic of ice and water. The black specks are hundreds of harbor seals, and some appear in danger, floating on icebergs beneath the towering wall of unstable ice. Yet this icy world is a major haul-out area—a safe refuge and birthing place for the seals.

Imagine a twenty-four-pound seal pup sliding from the womb onto a slab of ice, its new home. These warm-blooded mammals, sheathed in a thick layer of blubber, are well adapted for the shocking temperature change. A floating iceberg offers an ideal birthing platform and resting place, free of predators like killer whales.

Harbor seals in northern regions typically give birth in May and June. The pups grow rapidly, doubling their body weight in a month's time, suckling milk with a 45 percent fat content. Now, at the end of July, the pups are weaned and independent. It is difficult to distinguish the young from the adults, and each seal wears its own signature dappled fur coat. Some of the seals are buff with brown flecks, while others are tawny brown or ash-gray with black specks.

Moving quietly in a kayak, you can
sometimes see harbor seals eye to eye.

Undisturbed by humans or predators, harbor seals rest together on ice in front of Meares Glacier in Unakwik Inlet.

As we pass them, the seals rest peacefully on the ice, seemingly unaffected by our presence. Plump crescents, they balance on their bellies, hind flippers pointed up and forelimb flippers tucked at their sides. One can't help but stare into their eyes, deep indigo pools reflecting the ice around them.

Harbor seals are well adapted for hunting fish in cloudy glacial waters. Unlike whales and dolphins that use echolocation to find prey, harbor seals have highly sensitive long whiskers that detect the movement of prey that cannot be seen. Engineers at Massachusetts Institute of Technology report that blindfolded trained seals can follow the exact path of an underwater creature some thirty seconds after it swims past them. Their specialized whiskers interpret the wake's vibrations, revealing clues about the path, size, and shape of the prey.

A distant cracking sound commands our attention. "There it goes!" someone shouts.

In the distance we see a hundred-foot pinnacle of ice peel off the glacier's face in slow motion. Then there's a thunderous roar as the ice tower crashes into the water, sending a surging wave across the fjord. We stand spellbound, marveling at the power of glacial ice, while the kittiwakes swarm and dive into churning, milky water. Most of the seals continue resting, accustomed to the booms and rocking sea.

With great astonishment, we watch the Chenega Glacier calve and create upwellings rich with marine life, new ice floes for harbor seals, and more freshwater for our rising seas. In the face of climate change, I wonder how long these receding tidewater glaciers will last? And when all the ice has melted, what will become of our glacial seals?

OPPOSITE—*Ice floes provide a safe birthing and resting place for harbor seals.*

TOP—*Harbor seal on a small ice floe in Nassau Fiord near Chenega Glacier.*

Among Bears and Eagles

It's a breathless morning on McClure Bay. Layers of clouds and mist obscure the surrounding mountains, shrouding the rainforest in silence. The rhythmic stroking of paddles breaks the quiet as our kayak slips through the glassy intertidal water. Below, I spot small, purple shore crabs racing between barnacle-specked rocks, while gold rockweed undulates with the current. Every so often we see a dazzling orange or purple starfish, anchored in a sheltered pool.

On this particular day, I'm paddling with Kaz, an eighty-two-year-old woman on her first trip to Alaska. Fit and full of enthusiasm, this is also her first experience in a kayak, and she's thrilled to be paddling. A retired graphic designer, Kaz sees the beauty in rock and water, the intricate patterns of nature, and the subtle elements of a landscape few would stop to study and photograph.

"What's that?" Kaz hears a strange new sound.

It's the shrill, descending chitter of a bald eagle soaring above us. We watch it perch on the crown of a moss-cloaked Sitka spruce. We're close enough to see the intense golden eyes of this formidable bird. Kaz and I spot several bald eagles, some flying above the forest, others gazing down at us from their evergreen perches. When eagles gather near the head of a bay or an incoming stream, you can safely bet that salmon are there.

Soon we see salmon jumping and wriggling up a nearby shallow inlet stream. It's low tide, so we can clearly observe the big chum salmon (also known as dog salmon in Alaska because they are traditionally fed to sled dogs). They wiggle and scoot across the water's surface, dorsal fins and backs exposed. There are hundreds of them, moving through the shallows, thrashing and splashing to reach the clear freshwater inlet.

Without a whisper, Hugh points across the stream, near the forest's edge. We study the landscape of tall spruce and hemlock, alder thickets, and a fringe of meadow. Something round and dark is moving. A big

A black bear crosses a rushing river draining the steep-sided rainforest environment of Barry Arm, between Coxe and Barry glaciers.

black bear, looking healthy, with a belly no doubt full of salmon, ambles through the grasses and scattered willows. What a great place to scoop up a favorite fish.

This bear is one of few sighted on *Discovery* trips in recent years. Their numbers have dropped in the area because of increased hunting pressure, which includes the allowance of bear baiting. While black bears were once regularly seen along the streams and beaches of Prince William Sound, road access to Whittier and overhunting has diminished their population. A number of people have raised their voices about the worrisome decline, including Dean, who has witnessed it.

We watch the sleek bear with glossy, thick black fur swagger up the river in no particular hurry. Near the stream, there are thickets of salmonberries and blueberries, a perfect buffet for the bear. After he disappears in the woods, we beach the kayaks and take a closer look at the salmon as they muscle upstream through water just a few inches deep.

A bald eagle perches in a western hemlock tree in Cedar Bay.

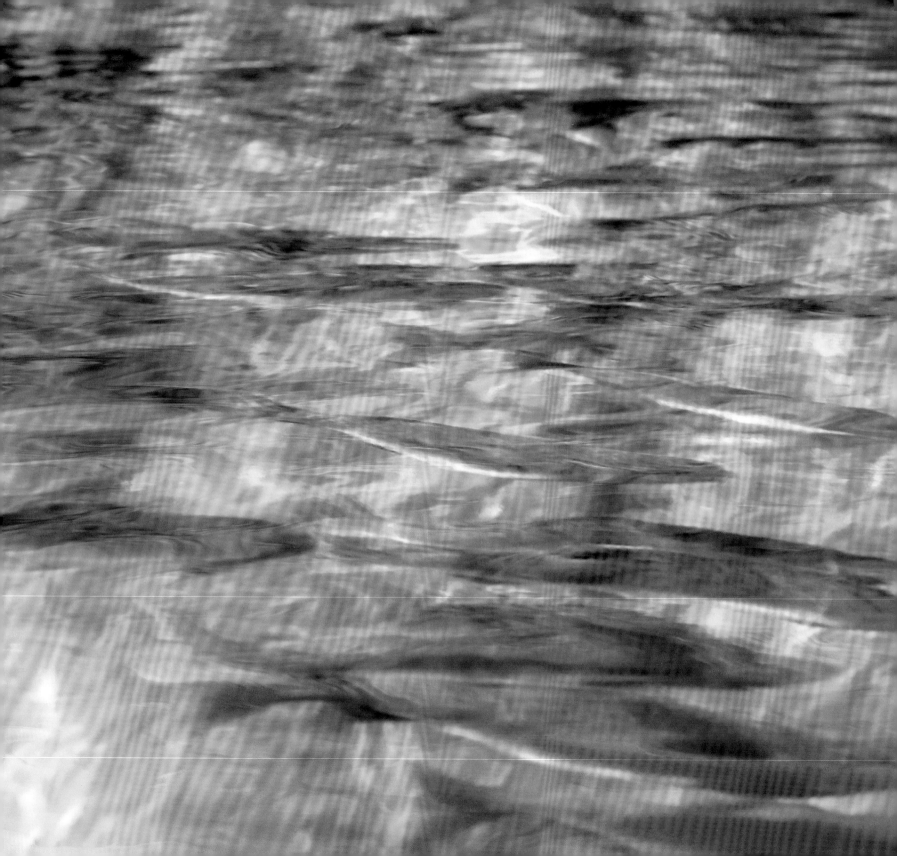

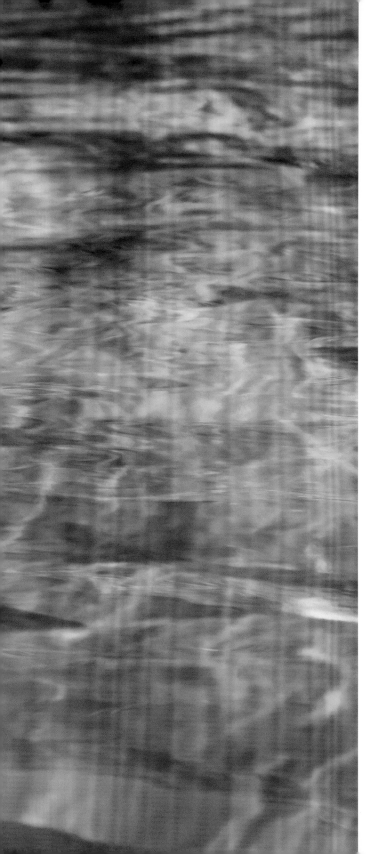

Salmon Encounter

Crouched on the riverbank, I'm looking into the eyes of several large chum salmon, their heads and slithering bodies well above the water. Chum salmon are hefty fish, second only to king salmon in size. The spawning males have hooked jaws with sharp, canine-like teeth. Their mouths gape as they fin their bodies forward. Some become stranded in the shallows. They twist, jackknife their bodies, and leap to reach deeper water.

The clear water of the stream offers a great chance to see these colorful fish. The males, some of them ten-pounders, have flashing plum stripes streaking across their silver-green bodies. Each fish has a unique psychedelic, tie-dyed pattern of colors. The females' coloring is more subdued, with a dark stripe running along the midline of their silvery bodies.

The countless streams around Prince William Sound support healthy salmon spawning runs, including four species of Pacific salmon: chum (dog), pink (humpback), red (sockeye), and silver (coho) salmon. Two major state-owned hatcheries in the Chugach wilderness also enhance pink and sockeye runs, largely for commercial fishing. While the hatcheries produce millions of fish for the commercial fishing industry, some worry that over time such fish will diminish the strength and productivity of wild salmon, and, in fact, some scientists argue that this is already happening.

These wild chum salmon are nearing the end of their lives. After spending three to four years at sea, they now return to their birthplace, the natal stream where we stand. Here the males and females will pair and spawn. In three to four months, their buried fertilized eggs will hatch. The tiny fry will spend a short time in the stream, then migrate to saltwater when they are one to two inches long. For several months, they will live in protected waters, hiding in eelgrass beds, eating insects and crustaceans, escaping bigger fish. When ready, the survivors will venture out into the big, deep blue.

Pink salmon school up in eelgrass beds in McClure Bay before migrating into freshwater streams to spawn.

This stream is pristine. Each fin, every rock, each wisp of algae is in perfect focus. It is one stream of thousands that flow into Prince William Sound from the glaciated mountains and through the dense forest. The temperate rainforest filters every raindrop through its moss-cloaked branches, its understory of devil's club and ferns, its thick sedge meadows, and its luxurious carpet of spongy sphagnum moss. This filtering creates the crystalline, pure, oxygen-rich water that spawning salmon need.

Each stream in the rainforest is a living thread connecting land to sea. What the stream and sheltering forest give to the salmon, the salmon give back when they return to their birthplace. The spawning salmon are a source of food for many forest creatures, and the marine nutrients from their decaying carcasses enrich the web of life in and around the streams. As much as 70 percent of the nitrogen found in vegetation near spawning streams comes directly from salmon. This means a Sitka spruce in salmon-spawning country can grow more than three times faster than trees living away from such streams.

Amy Gulick's book *Salmon in the Trees: Life in Alaska's Tongass Rain Forest* eloquently portrays this story. Just as salmon are *in* the trees, so are trees *in* the salmon. The leaves and needles of streamside plants provide shelter and food for invertebrates. Some of those tiny creatures fall in the water and become a salmon meal. When leaves, branches, or trees fall in a stream, they provide nutrients and food for bacteria, algae, plankton, and aquatic insects. Young salmon then thrive on these food sources. Each generation of salmon benefits from the nutrient-rich forest that their ancestors helped create.

Chum salmon vie for space to spawn in a river channel near upper McClure Bay.

WILDERNESS STEWARDS

One rainy morning, we approach Applegate Island to help clean up beaches and campsites. Tim and Barbara Lydon, US Forest Service wilderness stewards, lead the team of three college interns and me, all of us wrapped in rain gear and carrying yellow trash bags. The Lydons are passionate advocates of "leave no trace" camping, aspiring to keep the wilderness study area as wild as possible. Each year they check hundreds of islands and coastal sites to maintain the beauty and magnificence of a land married to the sea.

As we near the island on the Forest Service's *Dora Keen* we see two brightly colored jumbo umbrellas upright on the shore. Bob Hume and Peg Faithful are beneath them, veteran campers from Anchorage who have visited Prince William Sound each year for the past twenty years. Equipped with two single sea kayaks, Bob and Peg usually take three to four trips on the Sound per year, making it a point to explore a different area every summer.

It's pouring rain while we visit, and these two hardy campers are smiling and jovial, as if they take pleasure in the conditions. I ask them why they come back year after year, and they are exuberant in answering.

"Last night we saw the biggest surf roaring on the exposed side of the island. Three- to four-foot waves!" Bob tells us.

They had followed weather forecasts closely with a two-way radio and had paddled to a protected cove to escape the storm surge and gale-force winds. Tim had also maneuvered the *Dora Keen* away from the ripping winds, into a more sheltered bay. It would turn out to be one of the biggest storms of the summer.

Bob and Peg explain that each year they see different things, from breaching humpback whales to the rare glimpse of a wolf prowling the shoreline. The tides, weather, and wildlife are always changing. Bob, an attorney, and Peg, a software specialist, say they like to unplug from their busy city lives. During their treasured times in Prince William Sound, life is simpler. They focus

Peg Faithful and Bob Hume (Bob Hume)

on eating, paddling, and observing the spectacular surroundings. They love leaving the world of high technology and case law behind them.

"We've only seen one other kayak party during our ten-day trip," Peg says, with appreciation for the quiet time.

Bob and Peg love the wilderness character of the lands that surround Prince William Sound, and they make a strong effort to keep an immaculate campsite. In Anchorage, Bob has given workshops on the ethical practice of "leave no trace" camping. They are passionate wilderness advocates.

The rain begins to let up as we leave the two and scatter with bags in hand, combing the beaches for plastic, fish net remnants, and other debris. I walk through a grove of old-growth trees with a canopy so dense there is no trace of sky. The ground is luxuriously soft with wet moss that swallows my rubber boots. There is a peaceful, sacred quality to this dark green world, where the flutelike song of the hermit thrush echoes.

OPPOSITE—Moss covers rocks in the Eshamy River where it cuts through the rainforest.

LEFT—*Beached icebergs in the Nellie Juan Lagoon*

RIGHT—*Nellie Juan blue ice*

LEFT—*Harlequin ducks take flight from the rockweed beds on the moraine at Cannery Creek, Unakwik Inlet, where they were feeding.*

RIGHT—*A migrating surfbird stops to dine on barnacles and small snails and worms in Knight Island's rocky intertidal environment.*

LEFT—*A black bear skull overgrown with moss under the rainforest canopy, Eaglek Bay*

RIGHT—*The Meares Glacier, here encroaching on old-growth coastal temperate rainforest, is one of very few glaciers that have advanced in recent years.*

Tufted puffins gather on the cliffs of Glacier Island near their nesting burrows under the roots of old-growth hemlock and spruce.

A tufted puffin takes flight near Glacier Island.

TOP—A lion's mane jellyfish drifts in the shallow water of Copper Bay on Knight Island.

BOTTOM—Sunflower sea stars line the bottom of a well-protected tide pool in Copper Bay, Knight Island.

Low tide in Esther Passage
exposes creatures like this
leather star that lives in the
rocks among rockweed
and blue mussels.

On Bainbridge Island, upland peat bog environment blends with coastal temperate rainforest.

Fringed by blooming dwarf dogwood, the Cascade River drains glacial meltwater from high mountains between College Fiord and Eaglek Bay before feeding into Cascade Bay.

Journey Up College Fiord

Paddlers of the Past

On this calm, cloudless morning, the water looks like polished glass. Our paddles slice through beautiful reflections of College Fiord. This brilliant mirror features glaciers stair-stepping down to the shore, the evergreen forest spilling from the mountains into quiet coves, and countless waterfalls and streams plummeting to the sea.

College Fiord cradles the extraordinary wilderness of the Chugach National Forest in such sharp focus that one could mistake the reflection for the real land and sky itself.

I'm traveling with Richard Nelson (Nels), a cultural anthropologist and soundscape artist. We're surrounded by a vast, encompassing silence, broken only by the sound of our paddles and the rush of water cascading down the slopes. Our bright yellow sea kayak is streamlined but hefty. *Battleship Tango* weighs about ninety pounds when empty. We are on a two-week exploration trip, bound for the spectacular Harvard and Yale tidewater glaciers at the head of the fjord.

Passing the mouth of the Coghill River, we count fifteen harbor seals, diving and chasing after sockeye salmon that are heading up the river to spawn. Scores of tree swallows dive, dart, and slice through the air, snatching insects. You have to admire their graceful cursive

OPPOSITE—*Paddling into Yale Arm toward Yale Glacier at the head of College Fiord*

63

movements as they fly inches above the water, always in perfect control. One pair perches on a branch near the water, close enough that we can see their delicate faces.

Nels spent several years with Koyukon people in northwestern Alaska, documenting their traditions in his book *Make Prayers to the Raven*. "Koyukon people occasionally ate swallows, and the elders said that if a young woman drank the soup she would have beautiful children," Nels recalled as we paddled by Coghill Point, a forested peninsula that juts into the fjord like an index finger.

Coghill River and Coghill Point are historically important for fishing and as a seasonal subsistence campsite for the Chugachmiut—the Chugach people of Prince William Sound, also known as the Chugach Sugpiaq. At the time of European contact in the late eighteenth century, the Chugachmiut people numbered fewer than one thousand, and they depended on seals, sea lions, fish, and shellfish for much of their diet. Their eight territorial groups lived in a circle of winter villages and seasonal camps around the Sound.

As we paddle our kayak, I picture Chugachmiut people as they hunted seals or sea lions, traveling in their traditional double-holed boats known as *qayahpak*. Such a boat, also known by the Russian name *baidarka,* allowed the front paddler to fire an arrow, dart, or gun while the back paddler steadied the boat.

Building such a boat was a complex process involving both men and women. In *Looking Both Ways: Heritage and Identity of the Alutiiq People*, Native elder Bobby Stamp describes how the women on or around Prince William Sound scraped and cured seal and sea lion skins and sewed them together with thread made from porpoise sinew. The softened skins were tightly stretched over the boat frame that men made out of hemlock, alder, or spruce wood. The frame was lashed together with flexible spruce roots, rawhide, or sinew, so that the elegant boat would easily flex and flow with the waves.

For thousands of years, northern Indigenous peoples have explored and hunted along the North Pacific and Arctic coast using skin-covered boats. Today millions of people all over the world use kayaks for recreation, enjoying the same sleek boat design invented by the ancient ancestors of the Chugachmiut. Without the invention of the *qayahpak,* Nels and I would probably be rowing a dory.

The Mysterious Marbled Murrelet

Drifting among the reflections of this glacial landscape, I see two dark spots on the water that resemble quotation marks—a pair of marbled murrelets. These small, pudgy seabirds are shy and quick to dive or fly. As we approach, they take off with wings whirring, speeding along like bumblebees, just above the water. They've been clocked at sixty miles per hour. Occasionally we hear their muted *kerrr* calls.

Marbled murrelets spend most of their lives at sea, but instead of nesting in colonies like puffins and other members of the Alcid family, they are solitary, secretive nesters—so secretive that their nesting habits were a mystery to ornithologists for a long time. In fact, the marbled murrelet holds the distinction of being the last known bird species in North America to have one of its nests discovered.

Southern Alaska is home to most of the world's population of marbled murrelets, approximately three hundred thousand birds, yet the first documented nest was discovered in the coastal mixed redwood forest of Northern California by a tree trimmer named Hoyt Foster. In 1974, Foster was removing hazardous limbs on many trees that had been damaged by a freak snowstorm in Big Basin Redwoods State Park. One of those trees was a huge old-growth

OPPOSITE—A kayaker paddles past the enormous face of the Barry Glacier.

Douglas fir with enormous branches that sprawled over four campsites.

As Maria Mudd Ruth writes in her book about the marbled murrelet, *Rare Bird*, when Foster was 148 feet above the ground, he noticed a small, fluffy mass of feathers in a shallow depression of moss on a branch. In an effort to protect the unknown bird, Foster gently tried to capture it with a T-shirt. The chick didn't cooperate and fell to the ground, bouncing off mossy branches and landing on the soft forest floor unharmed. Park rangers and ornithologists would soon identify the web-footed seabird as a marbled murrelet.

Marbled murrelets depend on old-growth trees of the temperate rainforest for prime nesting habitat. They are a threatened species in British Columbia, Washington, Oregon, and Northern California due to habitat loss, pollution, and fishing net entanglement. While marbled murrelets are relatively abundant in places like Prince William Sound and Southeast Alaska, their overall population has been in decline in recent decades. Thousands of marbled murrelets died in the immediate aftermath of the 1989 *Exxon Valdez* oil spill, and the species has yet to fully recover in the region.

The half-pound, web-footed marbled murrelet depends on sand lance and capelin—the bright little fish they dive for, catch, and carry back to their chicks in the forest. They are equally dependent on the mossy branches of trees, like giant Sitka spruce, for precious nesting sites. Marbled murrelets show us that there is no border between forest and sea. It is all one world— land, water, and life interwoven.

Marbled murrelet females lay one egg on a sheltered, mossy branch of an old-growth tree, and the parents share incubation and feeding duties. (Nick Hatch, Pacific Northwest Research Station, USFS)

Marbled murrelets spend most of their lives at sea, but their nesting strategy differs from those of puffins and other Alcid family members in that they nest in the highest branches of old-growth trees.

A Time to Listen

"The view up glorious. Four cascading glaciers descending in jagged white torrents, strange, silent and seemingly motionless through the rich green furred pastures of mountain goats."

So wrote John Muir as he traveled up College Fiord on the Harriman Expedition in late June 1899. Nels and I can now see the four glaciers Muir described: Wellesley, Vassar, Bryn Mawr, and Smith, all grinding their way down the mountains, buffeted by alpine green tundra, falling in frozen motion toward the forested seashore. Members of the Harriman Expedition elected to name these and other glaciers after notable colleges on the East Coast.

With our warming climate these glaciers have receded since Muir's time so that now only the Bryn Mawr actively sheds icebergs into the fjord. Vassar has shrunk the most. Its landlocked snout is at least a mile from the water's edge. In the distance, I see the upper reaches of a rock dome, its base still locked in ice. A glacier has swept away the top half of the dome, exposing its sheer face. It resembles Half Dome in Yosemite.

What will this dynamic landscape look like in a thousand years? Did John Muir bear witness to the beginning of a geological drama that will someday be a new Yosemite?

As Nels and I move closer to Harvard Glacier, we hear the distant thunder of calving ice. There is a symphonic character to the landscape, with the constant background sound of dashing streams and cascades, punctuated by booms. We skirt brash but can't avoid some pieces that scrape and bounce against the kayak. Rounding a peninsula that juts into the fjord, the view suddenly opens to reveal an astonishing panorama. In every direction, glaciers reach down from the mountains. We've come to the Yale Arm of College Fiord, with expansive views of the Harvard and Yale glaciers.

We set up camp on a point with exquisite surroundings. After a hefty burrito dinner on the beach, we are bushed from paddling. As we listen, we grow accustomed to the varied sounds. We drift off to sleep to the intermittent thunder of calving ice.

Each glacier has a distinct voice. Bryn Mawr roars fiercely, only three miles away. Yale is soft-spoken, its muffled booms six miles away. When Harvard sheds ice about seven miles away, its thunderous rumble reverberates up the fjord. Periodically we hear the sudden sound of surf on our rocky beach—this follows a surge of waves from ice calving in the distance. The first time this happens we are fooled into thinking it's the rush of wings from a squadron of birds flying over the tent.

In the morning I sit on the beach and watch a mother sea otter diving for a meal while her independent pup explores icebergs that drift nearby. The pup claws its way onto a hefty berg, then playfully slides into the water. Then it tries to conquer a berg that is too steep and slippery. After a couple of failed attempts, the pup gives up and finds an indentation in the berg that forms a perfect backrest. The pup floats on its back, nestled up against the ice throne, perfectly content to drift with the berg.

Behind the tent, I walk through a thicket of alders and willows, listening to the voices of orange-crowned warblers, song sparrows, redpolls, and the yodeling of yellowlegs in the marsh. A family of common mergansers has formed a flotilla on the glassy pond. I count ten fluffy chicks, swimming single file behind their mother. They occasionally poke their heads underwater and

The Harvard Glacier descends from the high peaks of the Chugach Mountains into the head of College Fiord. Several other tidewater glaciers—including Smith, Bryn Mawr, Vassar, and Wellesley—descend from the west side of the fjord.

Bryn Mawr Glacier

A female merganser and her brood of chicks run over the water in Yale Arm.

take short dives. The chicks will stay with their mother for two months or longer before they can fly.

Common mergansers are sleek diving ducks, and the females have what appears to be a wild, rust-colored, Mohawk hairdo. Known as "sawbills," all merganser species are experts at catching fish on the serrated edges of their bills. Female common mergansers are particularly bonded to their birthplace. Scientists know through genetic testing that the females, like salmon, return to the place where they hatched. This makes me wonder: how many generations of mergansers have begun their lives on this pond, listening to the rumble of calving glaciers?

For two evenings at our Yale Arm camp we witness a convention of mergansers at precisely the same time, eight o'clock, just offshore. We count seventy-five to one hundred adult mergansers gathering in a tight group. As if on command, like the mass start of a marathon, the whole congregation starts running across the water, flapping wings and pattering feet, in a frenzy. They skitter over a mile of water, crossing Yale Arm without a pause. We can barely see them when they reach the other side. These molting birds, apparently unable to fly, leave a spreading wake of glistening tracks.

"*Akpaqrauyuq.*" Nels remembers the Iñupiaq Eskimo name for merganser, which translates to "runs on water." He has an incredible linguistic memory from his time living in the Arctic village of Wainwright as an anthropologist in the 1960s.

Were these molting birds searching for a safe communal roosting spot? Did they regularly join together for the one-mile crossing to avoid predators? Was there food on the other side? Mergansers are highly social and known to form large aggregations, but the precise reason for this one-mile dash, two evenings in a row, remains a mystery.

Looking west from College Fiord toward Vassar Glacier, a tidewater glacier that has retreated and become landlocked.

Hikers descend toward Yale Arm and College Fiord along a rocky ridge recently exposed by the retreating Yale Glacier. In the distance you can see a small island that was buried under hundreds of feet of ice less than one hundred years ago.

Birth of an Island

Hundreds of glaucous-winged gulls swarm above a recently exposed island, filling the air with a chorus of high-pitched chuckles. We beach our kayak in a quiet nook away from the nesting zone and scramble up the bare, polished bedrock to get a better view of Yale Arm.

This island was completely buried in ice when members of the Harriman Expedition explored the fjord back in 1899. We find deep striations in the sedimentary rock that look freshly etched, as though the glacier had chiseled these grooves yesterday. The Yale Glacier has receded several miles in recent decades, revealing this new predator-free island, ideal for nesting gulls and terns.

On the etched slabs are small middens of broken mussel shells and clamshells. The gulls drop these mollusks from the air, then extract the food from the cracked shells. It's astonishing to think that this island landscape, this perfect nesting and dining habitat, didn't exist a few decades ago. The Yale Glacier continues to recede, like nearly all glaciers in Alaska, constantly revealing newly exposed land.

Paddling closer to the Yale Glacier, we move quietly through the labyrinth of bergs, listening to the muffled hooting of harbor seals. Suddenly there is a flash of black on white. Two pigeon guillemots fly across the 150-foot high face of the glacier. They have scarlet feet and striking wing patches shaped like mittens. One of these beautiful seabirds has a silvery fish in its beak as they wing their way to a series of escarpments along the fjord. Guillemots use rock cavities for their nesting sites, and the escarpments offer plenty of nooks and crevices. The population of these seabirds has yet to fully recover from the oil spill due to a number of factors including nest predation by mink and the availability of high quality schooling fish in nearshore waters.

On the face of the glacier, a few hundred-foot-tall ice pinnacles, known as seracs, tilt precariously toward us. We keep a safe distance, listening and watching.

Between the rumbles and splashes, we hear the faint, nasal voice of the Kittlitz's murrelet—*kerrr, kerrr, kerrr.* Ahead they are diving amid the bergs, and I marvel at their ability to survive in such frigid, ice-choked waters. This small, half-pound bird has a waterproof jacket of feathers and a love for the tiny, rich, oily fish associated with tidewater glaciers.

These seabirds look much like the marbled murrelets that we saw along College Fiord, yet their feeding and nesting habits are very different. This species is married to the glacial world of Prince William Sound. They prefer the broken ice floes and turbid glacial milk for their dining environment. As ice-loving birds, they have large eyes and highly specialized vision for diving and feeding on invertebrates and fish in the cloudy water.

Like the marbled murrelet, the Kittlitz's murrelet is a solitary nester, but instead of choosing a moss-cloaked tree branch, this seabird picks a remote, barren talus slope, high in the mountains, usually within twelve miles of the sea. One olive egg is typically laid on bare, cold rock, often near snow or a glacier. Both parents take turns incubating the egg for about two weeks, traveling to and from their feeding areas. No other bird is so closely associated with tidewater glaciers. Some simply call them glacier murrelets to avoid pronouncing the name of the German zoologist, Heinrich von Kittlitz, who collected the first specimen during a Russian expedition in the 1820s.

There are advantages to remote nesting sites with fewer predators lurking. In a recent study of 156 radio-tagged Kittlitz's murrelets, scientists found that 91 percent of the nests were not accessible to humans by foot, even when the researchers got as close as possible with the help of planes and helicopters.

Yet the Kittlitz's murrelet is the most threatened of the twenty-two species in the Alcid family, which includes puffins, guillemots, auklets, and murres. A candidate for the Endangered Species List, they have a narrow range along the coastlines of Alaska and eastern Siberia, with an uncertain and declining population in the tens of thousands. The US Fish and Wildlife Service estimates that up to 15 percent of the Kittlitz's murrelets in Prince William Sound (from five hundred to more than one thousand birds) died in the immediate aftermath of the *Exxon Valdez* oil spill.

With the added impacts of climate change and the gradual loss of tidewater glaciers, will these glacier-loving murrelets be able to adapt and survive?

Ghost Forest

The wind is at our backs as we kayak down the west side of College Fiord. A thick layer of pewter clouds has changed the water from a milky jade to a dusty periwinkle, a stunning color against the gray and black beaches, dark green forest, and brilliant white gleam of glaciers.

Near Wellesley Glacier, we beach the kayak in a quiet cove and explore the rocky outwash of the glacier and the crescent-shaped beach. Nels discovers some mountain goat tracks along the shore, and I scan the ridges and precipices above the glacier looking for white flecks that might be the sure-footed creatures. All I spot are rocks. John Muir referred to these alpine tundra slopes as goat pastures, so perhaps he spotted goats here nearly 120 years ago. Amazing climbers that cling to rock cliffs, mountain goats love the alpine zone where they graze on sedges and other mountain vegetation during summer.

There are about thirty thousand mountain goats in the high coastal areas of southern Alaska. The Chugach Mountains around Prince William Sound are home to a small population near the northern edge of their range.

The tide is going out, helping us make good time on our longest paddling day: twenty-four miles. As we stroke down the magnificent fjord, I study the map and realize we are about ten miles away from the epicenter of the 1964 earthquake, the largest earthquake ever recorded in North America, with a magnitude of 9.2. This is the spot where the North American and Pacific plates collided with such tectonic force that some island shores, like those of Montague Island, were heaved up nearly forty feet, exposing tidal areas that would eventually become forested, abruptly closing off streams for spawning salmon. Some salmon would adapt by spawning in the intertidal zone.

Chenega Island was thrust fifty-five feet to the south. Underwater landslides created thirty- to forty-foot waves that bashed Whittier's docks and killed thirteen people. Not far from the Nellie Juan Glacier the McClure Bay cannery toppled, and three people died. The tsunami tragically destroyed the village of Chenega and heavily damaged the seaport town of Valdez. Fifty-six people died in these two communities.

As the Pacific Plate uplifted some shores, other locations dropped, as the entire landscape tilted, like a seesaw. In forests that fringed College Fiord, trees suddenly had their trunks and roots submerged in saltwater. These trees soon died, but they still stand as upright bleached skeletons, pickled and protected through the absorption of saltwater. These earthquake trees offer nesting habitat for bald eagles and perches for gulls, tree swallows, and other birds.

We paddle by this ghost forest through a spot where the water has magically turned to a Caribbean blue. A bald eagle soars across the fjord in front of our kayak, and our eyes follow this majestic bird to its large stick nest, cradled in the crown of a stark earthquake tree. With binoculars we see the heads of eaglets in the nest. Farther from shore we hear the chatty voices of white-winged crossbills that appear to be feasting on spruce cone seeds in the living forest.

From violent earthquakes to calving glaciers, from glacial milk to crystal streams, and from the living rainforest to a ghost forest, this is a dynamic landscape, constantly changing.

A mountain goat sheds its heavy winter coat during spring along Surprise Inlet, near Surprise Glacier.

Mountain goats in Nassau Fiord near Chenega Glacier come down to the high tide line to lick salt from the rocks.

Looking west from Golden
across College Fiord toward
Mount Gilbert and Mount Muir

The song of male orange-crowned warblers—chee chee chee chew chew— varies enough that individual males can be identified by the version they sing.

TOP—*Pacific wren in the forest at Coghill Point in College Fiord*

BOTTOM—*Tundra swans, migrating north, rest on the calm waters of Yale Arm, College Fiord.*

*A blue iceberg shed from
Yale Glacier floats in Yale
Arm on a rainy August day.*

"Nature is ever at work building and pulling down, creating and destroying, keeping everything whirling and flowing, allowing no rest but in rhythmical motion, chasing everything in endless song out of one beautiful form into another."

—*John Muir,* Travels in Alaska

Through the Eyes of John Muir

Reflections from the 1899 Harriman Expedition

Dean Rand focuses intently on the water as he carefully watches for bergs and navigates around them. We're in the wheelhouse of the *Discovery*, motoring up Barry Arm. The illuminated nautical screen reveals a peculiar map.

We are sailing on a phantom glacier.

The chart shows the *Discovery* moving across the Barry Glacier, over land for about three miles, when in fact our vessel is on water next to a recently exposed island. The nautical charts have yet to catch up with climate change and the retreating glaciers.

"There's Canada!" Hugh smiles on deck, pointing to a rocky island that is not on the map.

About a decade ago, the Barry Glacier and neighboring Cascade Glacier retreated to a point where new land began to emerge in the fjord. Suddenly an

OPPOSITE—*Barry Glacier face seen from a kayak on Barry Arm*

island of bedrock once buried by hundreds of feet of ice saw the light of day. Dean and Hugh witnessed the unveiling of this new land with astonishment. Hugh kayaked over to the island and jokingly claimed it for Canada, his birthplace. He was likely the first person to step on this mass of slate.

When the Harriman Expedition ventured up Barry Arm in 1899 and this island was buried in ice, the fjord was only half as long as it is today. The monstrous face of the Barry Glacier greeted John Muir, naturalist John Burroughs, and others on the *George W. Elder* at Point Doran, more than four miles away from where the *Discovery* now floats. At that historic juncture, there was a narrow inlet of open water between the glacier's face and the point. A great discussion commenced on whether it was safe for the steamship to proceed into uncharted waters through such a narrow passageway.

Captain Humphrey had refused to take the ship any farther. But expedition leader and sponsor Edward Harriman insisted that they try to explore the waters beyond the glacier. John Muir reflected in his journal: "Mr. Harriman ordered full speed ahead, rocks or no rocks. We saw a fine glacier and went within three hundred yards or so of the front. Ventured around the point on our left and saw another glacier; still venturing, we saw another and another, until the fifth glacier was seen discharging bergs into the main inlet, which is about fifteen miles long. Harriman, excited, said, 'We will discover a new Northwest Passage.'"

Harriman did not discover a Northwest Passage, but his scientific expedition was the

Mount Muir towers over Harriman Fiord
and a pond filled with lilies in late summer.

first to explore a new fjord that sharply turned south from Barry Arm, like a tern's wing in flight. It would be named Harriman Fiord in his honor. Muir would spend two days camping, exploring, and sketching the glaciers along this magnificent fjord.

Glaciers and their surrounding environment fascinated Muir. He was keenly observant of botanical features, describing every tree and flower in great detail. About a stand of impressive hemlock growing near the Harriman Glacier he wrote in his journal, "The first pure forest of Patton [western] hemlock I ever saw at sea-level. It seems old, storm-beaten, snow-crushed, yet strong and cheery and irrepressibly lovely in form, contriving to be beautiful under every condition of weather and soil or bare rock, bare save the cover blessed *Cassiope* [white mountain heather] spreads."

Muir studied one hardy hemlock that hunters had recently cut down. It was only nine inches in diameter, yet when Muir counted the rings he found it to be 325 years old, a testament to the endurance of these slow-growing trees at this latitude. Muir traveled with "Indian Jim" of Yakutat, who discovered old mossy stumps of trees cut by the Chugachmiut people as well as a recent hunting camp, where they spotted bear sign. While the Harriman Expedition was the first scientific exploration of the area, there was plenty of evidence that Indigenous people had journeyed here, slipping by the massive glacier near Point Doran in their *qayahpaks*.

Cascade Glacier tumbles down the side of Mount Gilbert and into Barry Arm at sunset. Cascade was a tidewater glacier until 2012, but has since retreated and is a "hanging" glacier today.

LEFT—*This view of Surprise Glacier is similar to Muir's but today Cataract Glacier has retreated and no longer reaches the sea.*

TOP RIGHT—*When John Muir camped along Harriman Fiord in 1899, he sketched this picture of Surprise and Cataract glaciers. At that time, both glaciers tumbled into the sea.*

BOTTOM RIGHT—*As the Harriman Expedition traveled up Barry Arm, John Muir sketched this scene of the Barry Glacier and the Chugach Mountains.*

Muir spent a considerable time sketching some of the dozen glaciers in Harriman Fiord. In this fjord, Muir and other team members named the glaciers by describing their physical appearance: Serpentine, Surprise, Stairway, Cataract, Roaring, Wedge, and Toboggan. Serpentine wraps around the mountains like a snake; Stairway is a steep, icy staircase rising from Surprise Glacier; Cataract looks like a frozen waterfall; and Roaring describes the constant sound of rushing waterfalls, thunderous calving, and crashing hunks of ice that fall from hanging glaciers, sometimes from cliffs as high as three thousand feet above the water. This was, and still is, one stupendous show.

Surprise Glacier

On board the *Discovery*, we move up Harriman Fiord, and I'm in awe of countless waterfalls and hanging glaciers that abruptly stop at the edge of cliffs above us. The mountain summits are shrouded in gray, swirling clouds. I try to imagine this fjord nearly sealed off by the Barry Glacier as it was during the Harriman Expedition. How astonishing it must have been when the expedition discovered such a major fjord with several tidewater glaciers. No wonder they named one of them Surprise.

Dean wheels the *Discovery* through a steady drizzle toward Surprise Glacier. The closer we come, the more amazing its colors and sounds. Waterfalls plummet down the mountains from unseen hanging glaciers, like white ribbons falling from all directions. Water and more water, steadily roaring into the fjord.

Surprise Glacier at sunset

Surprise Glacier flows into
Surprise Inlet in Harriman
Fiord. This glacier, along
with Cataract Glacier on the
left, flows from lofty peaks
that rise seven thousand
feet above the fjord.

We study the enormous face of Surprise, three hundred or more feet of fissured ice rising vertically from sea level, electric-blue seracs leaning every which way. Since it is a cloud-covered day, the ice appears more blue, as though someone has put a filter over the brilliant white ice. With less reflection due to the clouds, we can better see the short wavelengths of blue that are reflected by the dense ice.

The rampart face of the Surprise Glacier is really a convergence of two glaciers. Like a gravel road, the medial moraine sweeps down between them, a pathway of rock debris emptying into the sea. We listen to the Surprise crack and rumble, patiently waiting for a tower of ice to peel off and calve into the water. The rain is relentless, and all of us are dripping wet on deck, not wanting to miss a calving event. Turn away for a moment, and one might miss a skyscraper of jagged ice free-fall into the sea.

There is great beauty and drama in the falling rain, swirling mist, shrouded mountains, wild cascades, crumbling ice, and the otherworldly seracs, those massive ice pinnacles that lean perilously toward us.

Suddenly a boiling river of glacial silt explodes from the belly of the glacier. Massive hunks of ice tumble and roll in the torrent near the edge of the glacier's face. We watch in astonishment. The torrent is so powerful that in the span of a few minutes we witness the creation of a river delta. Waves of turbid water scoop up the till of the moraine and deposit it in braided piles. We watch this wild river craft a new gravel bar that fingers into the fjord. It feels like we are watching geological forces in a speeded-up time lapse.

I picture John Muir on the other side of the fjord, camped near the woods, with his pocket-sized journal

Serpentine Glacier flows off Mount Gilbert through ghost forests from the 1964 Good Friday Earthquake into the calm waters of Harriman Fiord.

on his lap. Muir made detailed pencil sketches of these glaciers and somehow managed to keep his pages clean and dry before the invention of waterproof storage bags.

As we leave the fjord the tide begins to ebb. In my mind's eye I see the Barry Glacier pressing toward Point Doran, almost blocking passage to Harriman Fiord. Then I imagine John Muir and John Burroughs on the deck of a steamship, long beards blowing in the wind, and I sense their excitement of traveling through uncharted waters. Leaving Harriman Fiord, Burroughs wrote:

> On coming out of the inlet and turning almost at right angles into Port Wells, the tide which was with us and which was running very strong, caught our vessel and for a moment held her in its grasp. She hesitated to respond to her helm, and was making direct for the face of the great glacier on our port side; but presently she came about, as if aware of her danger, and went on her way in less agitated water.
>
> This great glacier—the Barry—which guards the entrance to Harriman Inlet, presented some novel features; among others, huge archways above the water line, suggesting entrances to some walled city. When masses of ice fell I fancied I could hear the reverberation in these arched caverns.

Those caverns of Barry Glacier have now melted away, and this great glacier is now tucked around the corner. It is astounding to witness this new geography, these newly formed majestic fjords, and the pioneering trees that root themselves in rocks once buried by ice.

Cataract Glacier terminates on the mountainside above Surprise Inlet.

LEFT—The face of Barry
Glacier as viewed from
the top of "Canada"

RIGHT—Mount Muir

The calving front of Surprise Glacier

Islands

Sea Lions and Ravens

As the *Discovery* moves east toward Glacier Island, we pass towering cliffs that plunge into the sea. These prominent headlands resemble the prow of a ship. Rising about fifteen hundred feet above the breaking surf, the escarpments are visible from many vantage points in Prince William Sound.

Tucked beneath the cliffs, we see sausage-shaped creatures, their hulking bodies flung all over the rocky beach. Several hundred Steller sea lions have hauled out on shore, packed together, wedged between the cliffs and breaking surf. Glacier Island provides an important resting place for these endangered sea lions, first described by the German naturalist Georg Wilhelm Steller on Vitus Bering's Russian expedition.

When Steller landed on Kayak Island in 1741, just east of Prince William Sound in the Gulf of Alaska, he spotted a black-headed blue jay unfamiliar to him. At that moment Steller knew the expedition had reached a new continent. He and his shore party were the first Europeans to set foot in the place that would come to be known as Alaska.

In addition to his namesake, the Steller's jay, Steller observed five other species new to Europeans, including the Steller sea lion. He describes this formidable creature in *De Bestiis Marinis*, his chronicle of the voyage: "They far surpass the sea bear [polar bear] in strength and size. . . . They also give to the eyes and mind the impression of a lion."

Moving closer to the island, we spot several horned puffins bobbing in the waves, seabirds whose clownish faces make you stare, as though you are seeing a new cartoon character. I marvel at their massive orange and yellow beaks and wispy horns erupting from their eyelids. Most of the world's horned puffins breed in Alaska, and the cliffs of Glacier Island have many caves

OPPOSITE—*A raven, always the trickster, harasses Steller sea lions at Bull Head on Glacier Island.*

and crevices offering nesting sites for puffins, pigeon guillemots, and murres.

The deep bass grumbles of the sea lions grow louder, and we hear the bellows, belches, and lion-like roars of these blubbery giants. Most of them bask or snooze, shoulder to shoulder. Hugh likes to think of them as "a big pile of puppies," as some drape their tawny brown bodies over each other, but they are enormous, with the heaviest bulls weighing as much as twenty-four hundred pounds. The Steller sea lion is the largest eared seal among fourteen species in the world.

Some of the bigger bulls jostle with necks out-stretched, roaring and growling at each other. One impressive bull basks on a rock pedestal fringed by splashing surf. His massive chest bulges, and he holds his head high and aloof, eyes confidently closed. Such an imperial posture demands respect. And to think that during the nineteenth century their whiskers were sold, a penny apiece, for pipe cleaners.

Sea lions are an important resource for Chuga-chmiut subsistence. The Indigenous people tradition-ally used their thick, tough skins for clothing, boots, and coverings for their *qayahpaks* and *baidarkas*. They also ate the meat and burned sea lion fat in oil lamps for light and warmth.

This western population of Steller sea lions has declined dramatically on the Alaska Peninsula since the 1970s. It is not known why. One theory suggests that warming oceans have altered fish distribution and that populations of desired prey—small oily fish—have diminished. Such a diet change could cause nutritional stress for the sea lions. To better protect this endan-gered population, ocean waters near some of the key rookeries have been off-limits to trawl fishing, and sci-entists continue to carefully monitor the population.

On this warm summer day, most of the sea lions on this sheltered beach in the wilderness study area are resting, but suddenly the mood changes. Two ravens fly overhead, then descend and land on a driftwood log, just above the loungers. Immediately the sea lion heads pop up in response, and I hear a rumbling chorus. Some sea lions scoot into the water, while others ripple their way down the beach, distancing themselves from the ravens. Comically, it seems like the ravens are herding the huge beasts.

One sea lion seems particularly annoyed. He turns and lunges at one of the ravens, growling. The raven puffs up its feathers, with wings half-outstretched. Am I imagining this faceoff? No, this is a real-life, if unusual, David and Goliath showdown, but the raven soon retreats, hopping away from the roaring bull. Meanwhile, the other sea lions have moved away from the ravens, many into the water.

For whatever reason, this herd of hundreds of sea lions reacted as though a major predator lurked. Maybe Raven, the legendary trickster, just decided to create a little havoc for a bunch of burly, one-ton beasts.

OPPOSITE TOP—*A Northwestern crow perches in a Sitka spruce in the coastal temperate rainforest. (Debbie Miller)*

OPPOSITE BOTTOM—*When German naturalist Georg Steller landed, in 1741, on Kayak Island, just east of Prince William Sound in the Gulf of Alaska, he spotted a black-headed blue jay unfamiliar to him and knew the expedition had reached a new continent. The Steller's jay bears his name.*

RIGHT—*Curious subadult male Steller sea lions gather to investigate a boat near the Bull Head Steller sea lion haul-out on Glacier Island.*

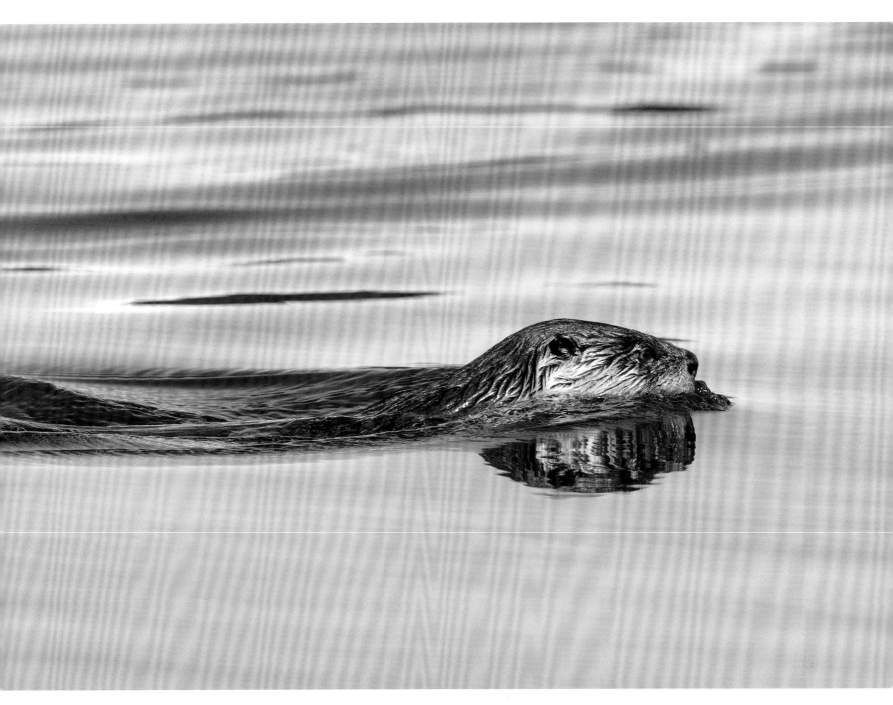

River otter swimming in Eaglek Bay

Peat Bogs, River Otters, and Flowers in Profusion

Dean finds shelter in Chamberlain Bay near Glacier Island. He anchors the *Discovery* in a quiet cove rimmed with a gravel beach that shows the strata of changing tides. Glistening amber-gold rockweed, a common seaweed, reveals the most recent tide line. Farther up the beach, reddish brown lines of dried seaweed encircle the shore like bathtub rings. Above the highest line of seaweed and driftwood, light green succulents emerge, buffeted by tall beach grass. Beyond the grass, lush alder thickets and devil's club fringe the dense rainforest of spruce and hemlock.

There is beauty in this layering of subtle colors and textures—from the slick green-blue waters of the bay to the wispy, white-bearded lichens that stream from the crowns of moss-cloaked Sitka spruce.

On the north side of Glacier Island, we've entered a quiet, beautiful wilderness, far from the roaring sea lions and crashing surf. Guided by Hugh and Dean, and by Heather Rand, Dean's daughter, I'm strolling with others through a squishy peat bog near the edge of the forest. By a stroke of luck, this wetland meadow is in full bloom in late July, with splashes of color woven through the deer cabbage, skunk cabbage, sedges, and grasses. We walk on a lush carpet of thick, spongy moss speckled with a profusion of blooming wildflowers. Heather has grown up on Prince William Sound and points to flowers, naming them as though it's her backyard: purple iris, magenta shooting stars, chocolate lilies, lavender daisies, swamp gentian, beach pea, lousewort, and the delicate plumes of white bog orchids. These orchids make you pause, kneel, and smell their sweet, intoxicating fragrance.

Pond lilies in an upland peat bog pond at North Esther Passage, College Fiord

We skirt a couple of ponds, sparkling dark pools dappled with yellow pond lilies. Well-worn narrow trails stitch the ponds together. A closer look reveals the tracks of river otters. On a clump of moss we discover fragments of mussel shells and fish bones deposited by an otter. Hugh notes that river otters, like bears and eagles, bring a significant amount of marine nutrients into the rainforest, fertilizing the environment.

Like the sea otter, the river otter has webbed feet and belongs to the weasel family. But the smaller river otter can run faster than a human and is an excellent swimmer. I once caught a close glimpse of this agile creature as it moved across barnacle-crusted rocks, fetching Pacific blue mussels at low tide. The graceful motion of its slinky, elongated body was liquid. With his back arched high, his undulating body formed ribbon-like loops as he moved across the shore.

Dean points to the open root structure of an old hemlock where there appears to be a sheltered, mossy cavern in the base of the tree. He explains that river otters like to live beneath such root structures in dens, and there is plenty of evidence that Glacier Island hosts a healthy otter population.

I think of animals—like river otters, sea lions, and seabirds—that have no boundaries between land and sea. These creatures rely on both earth and ocean for their home in order to survive. A coast is not a line of separation but rather a seam that binds the aquatic and terrestrial worlds together. It is *one living mosaic* of forest and glaciers, islands and fjords, ponds and peat meadows, rivers and lakes, beaches and spits, moraines and underwater sills, tide pools and mud flats—all woven together.

A waterfall cascades from a small glacier
toward the fucus-covered intertidal
area of Esther Pass in Waterfall Bay.

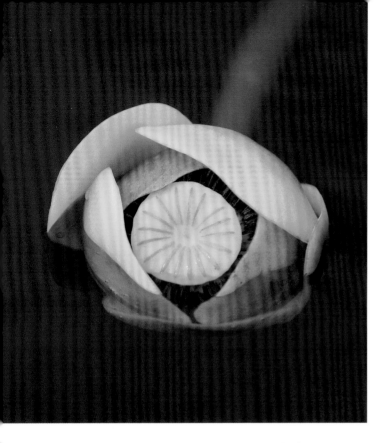

TOP LEFT—*Wild iris growing in the upland peat bog environment, Bainbridge Island*

TOP RIGHT—*Western columbine blossom on Ingot Island*

BOTTOM—*Butterwort, a carnivorous flowering plant, grows on a glacial moraine at Columbia Glacier, in mid-June.*

PREVIOUS PAGE, TOP LEFT—*Yellow pond lily, North Esther Passage, College Fiord*

PREVIOUS PAGE, BOTTOM LEFT—*Blueberry blossoms in spring near Jackpot Bay, western Prince William Sound*

PREVIOUS PAGE, RIGHT—*Dwarf dogwood grows around the base of a western hemlock in Long Bay near Columbia Glacier.*

Alone

Surrounded by beauty, I'm alone on a nameless islet in Prince William Sound. This small, forested island is one of hundreds scattered across the Sound. From a distance, these tiny islands often look rounded, as though someone manicured the forest canopy into a perfect green dome.

Early this morning Tim and Barbara Lydon motored off on the thirty-foot aluminum *Dora Keen*, leaving me here to explore, reflect, and write. The Lydons are passionate about protecting the extraordinary values of the wilderness that surrounds Prince William Sound, including the Nellie Juan–College Fiord Wilderness Study Area. From the mountains, glaciers, and alpine meadows to the rainforest, peat bogs, shorelines, and hundreds of islands that dot the Sound, they have a huge region to take care of, and they love every minute of it.

Together with the Lydons and three Forest Service interns, I've just experienced an action-packed week of cleaning up campsites, collecting lichens for an air quality project, chatting with visitors, and checking pristine lakes for invasive elodea, a dominating aquatic plant that can strangle native species and destroy the natural lake environment. The sampling team fortunately found no evidence of this troublesome alien.

While this was a busy week in the field, it only reflected a fraction of the work required to maintain the area's wilderness character. On any given day, Barbara and Tim might be responding to reports of illegal structures, a messy bear bait station, or issues relating to the twenty-four commercial guides and

Layers of clouds fill the sky over Lucky Bay on the south end of Knight Island and the perfectly calm waters of Knight Island Passage.

outfitters who are permitted to work in the wilderness study area. The active stewardship of the Lydons and their caring for the area clearly demonstrate the importance of safeguarding this magnificent place so worthy of permanent wilderness protection.

Walking along the high tide line, I pace off the perimeter of the islet, following a rusty brown fringe of dried rockweed, a demarcation line between the intertidal world and the beach grasses and forest. The islet is two hundred steps in length and about sixty-five steps at its widest point. The inner forest of spruce and hemlock is lush, intimate, and compact, a miniature rainforest surrounded by the sea. Narrow and steeply angled, the pebbly beach connects these two worlds.

In a large, quiet tide pool, something reddish purple flashes near submerged rocks. Moving closer, I see a cluster of sunflower sea stars, one of the largest sea star species in the world, with arms that can span more than three feet. These creatures are magnificent in shape, texture, and color, and most have sixteen tenacious arms, although some can grow as many as twenty-four. Frequently they are joined arm to arm, with bodies overlying one another. Smaller sea stars are reddish, while larger individuals are lavender and purple, some with an underlying reddish core that resembles the color of magma. I count fifteen of them.

One particularly large sea star is hidden by a blade of kelp. I carefully peel it back only to discover another red sea star clinging to the underside. It creeps underwater using the tiny, anemone-like "tube feet" beneath each arm, grabbing on to rocks and plants in slow motion. The shape of this beautiful creature reminds me of Prince William Sound, with its many fjords, arms, and inlets reaching in all directions. Unlike those in many other areas along Alaska's coast, these healthy sea stars have apparently escaped the wrath of sea star wasting, an epidemic that has wiped out many populations in recent years.

Sunset light streams through broken clouds over the Chugach Mountains at the mouth of Eaglek Bay, Point Pellew, in late summer.

Along the shore, a flock of Northwestern crows has discovered a partially submerged driftwood log covered with gooseneck barnacles. Intelligent and opportunistic, the crows pick, pry, and pull the long fleshy appendages from the barnacles. From a distance it looks like the crows are stretching taffy from the log. While these social birds squawk and feast in the intertidal zone, song sparrows and chestnut-backed chickadees dart in and out of the forest. These coastal birds also love intertidal areas, feeding on insects and crustaceans in the heaps of rockweed, kelp, and other species of seaweed that are gifts from the tide.

When it starts to drizzle, the forest canopy becomes a natural umbrella. In the shelter of a regal Sitka spruce, I lean against the mossy trunk, as soft as a cushion. Up above me, a chestnut-backed chickadee tucks into a clump of moss that looks like a nest. These cheery birds use a blanket of moss to cover their eggs when they leave the site to feed.

Beyond the understory of devil's club and ferns are remnants of a small cabin or cache that have sunk into the mossy floor of the forest. Most of the structure has decomposed. Not far from salmon streams, this was perhaps someone's seasonal fishing camp. In the distance I hear a boat heading toward Main Bay, where the pink salmon are running. Commercial fishers are busy setting their drift nets at the entrance of the bay, not far from one of two fish hatcheries in the wilderness study area.

As the rain squall passes, I return to the beach and find each peak of the Chugach Mountains brilliantly illuminated, each distant glacier revealed. This majestic, serrated line of peaks and ridges sweeps across the northern horizon, rising up from cobalt blue waters like floating mountains. Such a majestic view commands

On a still summer morning, the calm waters of Long Bay reflect the morning fog and nearby trees.

attention. While I study the incredible topography of the Sound, black oystercatchers deliver their piercing, rapid-fire calls, and a harbor seal curiously watches me, head above the water, glistening eyes focused.

There is something magical about being alone on an island, where you can study wildness, reflect and quietly ponder, and better appreciate each blade of kelp, tide pool creature, gooseneck barnacle, mossy branch, singing bird, curious seal, and a surrounding view that leaves you spellbound.

The Heart of Knight Island

From the air, Copper Bay is shaped like a perfect heart. From a boat, this secluded bay is surrounded by a wilderness that is so majestic it could be its own national park.

"This jewel of a bay says it all," Tim Lydon declares, as he cuts the engine of the *Dora Keen*. We've entered a quiet, enclosed space, "screened by the topography," as he describes it. Tucked behind the mountains, there is no hint of passing boat noise that might be heard in the outside channel. Instead we listen to the cascading song of the hermit thrush, the splashing of salmon leaping out of the water, the cries of gulls feeding on salmon carcasses, the chitter of a bald eagle, and a distant family of crows squabbling over something.

Within this natural amphitheater, sheer rock walls rise up from one side of the bay and terraced meadows reach up slopes on the other side, with knife-edged peaks looming above. This bay reflects the character of wilderness in a grand way, from the iconic peaks that are landmarks for boaters across the Sound, to the alpine meadows that beckon climbers, to the fringe of rainforest that invites visitors to explore. In close proximity to the sea, all of these environments are within reach.

The intrinsic values of a truly wild landscape are here in these unnamed mountains, untrammeled meadows, and pristine waters, home to salmon and bears. The Chugach wilderness is a place of inspiration, holding the deep quiet and peace, allowing a person to explore, discover, ponder, and dream. This glorious spot on Knight Island is clearly one of the most beautiful and wild in the study area, but in the past the Forest Service has recommended against permanently protecting Knight Island, deferring to its potential value for mining. Others point out that existing wilderness values pump revenue into communities, where water taxis, tour operators, and guides bring many visitors from all over the world to experience this coastal wilderness.

Tim's purpose for visiting Copper Bay is to assess the area's potential as legally designated wilderness. He will study the map and landscape, analyze opportunities for recreation in a primitive area, and contribute his findings in a report that could ultimately spur congressional action.

The thought of mining or a major oil spill in such a dazzling wilderness is appalling. Yet history shows that these things have happened and could happen again unless we do all we can to safeguard Knight Island, a precious place in the Nellie Juan–College Fiord Wilderness Study Area.

Knight Island's unique geology of ophiolite, uplifted ocean crust, causes its mountains to tower precipitously.

OYSTER DAVE

Dean Rand steers the *Discovery* across Eaglek Bay toward a small floating dock surrounded by neat rows of buoys. David Sczawinski's eyes light up as he greets us with the enthusiasm of a hearty outdoorsman who loves his work on the water. Tall and robust, Dave has the core strength of a guy who has lifted hundreds of heavy containers of oysters out of Prince William Sound for more than twenty-five years.

Dave is the northernmost oyster farmer in America. He is passionate about growing oysters, eating them, and selling about thirty thousand of them each year at the annual Alaska State Fair, one of his outlets. He experiments with recipes: oyster burritos, oyster chowder, oysters with sour cream and salsa. He cooks them to perfection for customers who come back year after year to his Pristine Products Oyster Booth.

Most of his baby oysters, known as spat, come from the Pacific Northwest. These tiny Japanese oysters are about one-quarter inch long. He raises these filter feeders in thousands of stacked trays that are porous and oxygenated. The trays attract mussels that tenaciously grab on to the containers, and predatory starfish slide into the cracks and slip their arms around the oysters. Dave is resigned, willing to share the bounty.

It's not always easy. There are calamities. One year his vessel, the *Bumblebee*, almost sank after a winter storm dumped three feet of heavy, wet snow. Dave managed to rescue the boat using air bags to raise it, but some of his equipment was destroyed. The *Bumblebee* still floats but needs work on the hull because of marine worms boring holes through the wood. Dave sighs, raising his eyebrows, as if to say this just comes with the territory.

Dave pulls up a stack of trays. He shows us a batch of adult four-year-old oysters that have baby ling cod and other small fish and crabs mixed with them. The oysters have a frilly outer shell protecting their prized flesh. Occasionally Dave finds pearls. "I keep them in a plastic container for my retirement," he says, grinning.

"Oyster Dave" holds oysters grown in stacked trays on his oyster farm, Pristine Products, in Eaglek Bay.

Two salmon hatcheries and Dave's operation are permitted in the wilderness study area under the 1980 Alaska National Interest Lands Conservation Act. This monumental law set aside more than one hundred million acres of national parks, wildlife refuges, and forests, with allowance for certain traditional activities and uses on these federal public lands. Dave's oyster farm is an example of a sustainable business that can thrive on the fringe of this magnificent wilderness where land meets sea.

Just east of Prince William Sound, Kayak Island is where European explorers first set foot in Alaska, during the Vitus Bering expedition of 1741.

OPPOSITE—*Endangered Steller sea lions haul out in large numbers at Bull Head on Glacier Island.*

RIGHT—*Steller sea lions on a blue iceberg drifting off Bull Head on Glacier Island*

A small rock islet in Copper Bay along Knight Island is home to a miniature rainforest environment.

A Dall's porpoise breaks the perfectly calm surface of Knight Island Passage, as it bow rides off the M/V Discovery.

Where Is the Columbia Glacier?

Vanishing Glacier

Our inflatable raft fights the current as we make our way toward a peninsula that juts into Columbia Bay. The tide rushes out, surging through a narrow inlet. Tim Lydon paddles hard, as though he's in training. A few feet forward, a few feet back. Glaucous-winged gulls cry and circle above us as we reach the intertidal zone.

"This is it!" Tim exclaims. "Welcome to the terminal moraine of the Columbia Glacier," he says with breathless, boyish excitement.

With Sebastian Zavoico, a summer intern from Middlebury College in Vermont, Tim is on a Forest Service work trip, checking campsites, meeting visitors, and cleaning up beaches.

OPPOSITE—*The face of the Columbia Glacier as seen from a small nunatak—an isolated peak of rock projecting above a surface of inland ice or snow—that emerged from the glacier face in 2014*

123

Anxious to gain a view of one of the world's fastest retreating glaciers, we beach the raft, securing the line to an alder. We pick our way across barnacle-crusted rocks, bright clumps of gold rockweed, and clusters of blue mussels. The soft peeping of semi-palmated plovers and piercing cries of black oystercatchers announce that we've entered their territory.

Climbing the moraine, we step on boulders and cobbles that once called the mountains home, only to be gouged away, pushed, and deposited in this ridge. The immense mass of the Columbia Glacier carved, scooped, and carried enormous quantities of silt and rock from mountains to sea. Some of the larger boulders show striations where the belly of the glacier chiseled the rock, like old tire tracks in hardened mud.

There is a dynamic feeling in the air that this landscape was just created—a few minutes ago in geologic time.

Soon we stand on the high point of the moraine, about one hundred feet above sea level, and it's an astounding view. Floating icebergs of all shapes and sizes are scattered across the bay and up the fjord, but there is no sign of the largest tidewater glacier in Prince William Sound.

Dense, low-lying clouds obscure the spectacular peaks at the head of the bay, some rising to twelve thousand feet above the water. With binoculars I spot the distant edge of a tributary glacier spilling down from the clouds. That curving glacier once merged with the Columbia but now plummets into the water. The receding Columbia is hidden, tucked behind a prominent ridge known as the Great Nunatak.

In 1980 the two-hundred-foot-high visible face of the massive Columbia Glacier would have nudged my feet, but that mantle of ice has since vanished. The Columbia has retreated more than twelve miles from where I stand, leaving a twelve-hundred-foot-deep fjord in its astonishing track. Water has replaced ice.

Alders fringe the water on recently exposed land. Rock striations appear freshly scored.

Roughly forty square miles of this incredibly thick ice have melted. Disappeared.

Triggered by climate change and warming temperatures, the Columbia continues to shed a phenomenal amount of ice into the fjord. Studies by NASA and others report that the thickness and volume of the glacier has shrunk by half since 1980, losing about two cubic miles of icebergs each year through calving. This yearly loss of ice, bound for the ocean, holds five times more freshwater than the entire state of Alaska uses annually.

Recent work by glaciologists reveals that 50 percent of annual freshwater runoff into the Gulf of Alaska comes from glaciers and that glacier mass loss in the coastal temperate rainforest is among the highest on Earth, equal to the annual discharge of the Mississippi River. That is a lot of melting.

A few years after the 1899 Harriman Expedition, a Captain Johansen of the Alaska Commercial Company drove the steamer *Dora* by the Columbia Glacier. In 1902, he described the immense face of the glacier being six hundred feet above the water and six hundred feet below the surface. He cautiously steered the ship no closer than three hundred yards from the face because of the "immense bergs continually breaking," noting that "the waves made the ship roll heavily." Johansen also noted the beauty of the glacier's face, particularly at sunset. The low-angle light of the setting sun created a "wonderful play of prismatic colors" against the dark, forested mountains.

Looking across the bay, I see a procession of icebergs drift with the ebbing tide on their slow journey to the sea. They follow the U-shaped path of the glacier down the gouged three-mile-wide, fifteen-mile-long fjord. Some icebergs are the size of houses. Others, the size of cars, are known as growlers. These can unexpectedly roll or somersault, growling as they turn. Kayakers, beware.

Glacier scientist Austin Post studied and photographed Alaska's glaciers for more than two decades. In the early 1970s he predicted the retreat of the Columbia and warned of the danger of floating icebergs in shipping lanes, particularly for oil supertankers en route to and from Valdez.

As Post predicted, it was floating ice from the Columbia that drifted into the outbound shipping lane near Valdez on March 24, 1989. The supertanker *Exxon Valdez* changed course to avoid a collision and, due to careless navigation, hit Bligh Reef. The single-walled hull split open like a pop can, spilling eleven million gallons of poisonous crude oil into the clean, rich waters of Prince William Sound. Nearly thirty years later, the Sound continues to recover from this catastrophe and its lingering effects.

Power of a Snowflake

On this cloudy day, the colors of the icebergs are surreal. The glacial blue is an electric, otherworldly shade that seems to glow from within the bergs. It's hard to fathom that billions upon billions of snowflakes gave birth to what we now see as ice.

These floating ice sculptures were once part of the largest tidewater glacier in Prince William Sound. Imagine an immense river of ice, a glacier as thick as three thousand feet, just over half a mile deep. This enormous ice slab formed near the lofty peaks of the Chugach Mountains. This spectacular coastal range arcs around Prince William Sound and forms the perfect mitt to catch snow from the many winter storms that sweep across the North Pacific, plastering the mountains.

Just how much snow formed this glacier? As a raven flies, the upper reaches of the now-thirty-two-mile-long Columbia Glacier are only fifteen miles west of Valdez, a community that receives the most snowfall of any sea-level town in the world—an astounding twenty-five feet per year.

The surrounding Chugach Mountains top Valdez with an annual average of about fifty feet, one of the snowiest regions on Earth. Snowflakes here are big and wet, the kind of snow that binds together for the perfect snowball. Over time the flakes compress and turn into dense layers of ice that created the Columbia and twenty other major tidewater glaciers in Prince William Sound.

Yet even with this annual plastering of snow, coastal glaciers are melting and rapidly shrinking in a warming world. A recent aerial study reveals that nearly all of Alaska's coastal glaciers are receding, creating new landscapes in their wake and contributing to global sea-level rise. Of those coastal glaciers, the Columbia has lost about half of its ice thickness since 1980 and is one of the fastest-retreating glaciers in the world.

A Living Moraine

During cooler years past, when the Columbia accumulated more snow and ice than it lost, the glacier marched toward the Sound, plowing its way to Heather Island, near the mouth of Columbia Bay. Over time, the glacier's weight and unimaginable force scooped out a fjord twelve hundred feet deep. That same glacial tilling created a new landscape in the form of spits and shoals, peninsulas and islands, underwater moraines, and a sheltered cove where today I hear a common loon yodeling.

On this moraine I am surrounded by a young landscape. The pioneering alders, some waist-high, are at home in these rocky soils. They attract song sparrows that flit from shrub to shrub. Tenacious willows creep across the rocks between clumps of green moss and white, frilly lichens. Interspersed with this sparse vegetation are stunted Sitka spruce trees that look

OPPOSITE—A grounded iceberg from the Columbia Glacier sits on the tidal flats of Columbia Bay.

The Columbia Glacier as it looked thirty-five years ago (© 1983 Randy Brandon/Third Eye Photography)

The glacier today. Columbia Glacier has retreated more than twelve miles in the last thirty years, leaving behind the large and deep Columbia Bay.

Lupine on the terminal moraine of the Columbia Glacier in June

uncomfortable. These tiny trees are pale green and appear nutrient-deprived, as though they sprouted in the wrong place.

Much of this terminal moraine is submerged and invisible. It once helped stabilize the glacier, like a foot-rest, until the toe of the glacier fell off. Today's navigational depth charts show the moraine as a smiling curve across the entrance to the bay, five hundred feet high in some places. Boaters must be careful, particularly at low tide, to avoid shallows where they might collide with the moraine.

This underwater ridge of glacial deposits, known as a sill, produces upwellings that benefit foraging seabirds such as mergansers, loons, and kingfishers. With each tidal exchange, the sill creates a rich mixing zone like that at the calving front of a glacier. As the glacial freshwater flushes over the sill, it stirs up nutrients and fosters the growth of plankton, krill, small fish, and pteropods—little snails that swim with winged feet. An entire web of life benefits from this churning of waters.

Gulls and terns establish colonies on the moraine to feed their chicks with abundant small fish. Seals and sea lions dive near the sill for desirable foods like pollock and salmon. Humpback whales gorge themselves on krill and small fish. The Chugachmiut people still collect eggs on the moraine and fish and hunt as their ancestors have for centuries. Tim Lydon thinks of these glacial moraine zones as "biological hot spots."

In the spring and fall the moraine is a pit stop and staging area for migrating cranes, swans, long-tailed ducks, and other birds. To the casual observer, a moraine may look like a pile of rocks or a berm of sparsely vegetated scree. In reality moraines and underwater sills offer significant habitat for many creatures, including one of my favorites, the sea otter.

In May, surfbirds feed in the rocky intertidal environment of Columbia Bay while migrating north to their Arctic breeding grounds.

As the tide ebbs, I count twenty-four sea otters floating on their backs in the intertidal zone near the moraine. The table is set on their bellies, and they feast on shellfish. Some of them have a chosen rock that becomes a perfect centerpiece, and they use this anvil to crack open big clams. One mother otter holds a clam with her cat-like paws and pounds it on the rock. After several raps, the shell cracks, and she extracts the nutritious meat with her teeth and tongue.

Sea otters also use smooth, flat stones as tools for prying abalone off submerged rocks. Abalone shells can be extremely difficult to remove from their footholds. Where a human diver might use a special pry bar, sea otters chip away and bash the shells until the animal loses its hold or the shell breaks. Glenn Van Blaricom, who has studied sea otters for decades, once observed an otter make more than twenty consecutive dives in the same spot, each time surfacing with the tool rock tucked under its forelimb. With great perseverance, the otter finally surfaced with its abalone meal.

Meeeeee! The cry of an otter pup carries across the water. Just as the mother otter finishes her meal, her pup arrives and circles her, then climbs aboard. The playful pup sits upright on mother's belly as though it is on an island. Then it somersaults while mother floats with ease like a well-balanced raft. Otter pups are the champions of cuteness.

The sea otter is the smallest marine mammal in North America and the only otter capable of spending its whole life at sea. Amazingly, it has no blubber. Instead the otters rely on thick, luxurious fur, the densest of all mammals, with as many as one million hairs per square inch. To touch otter fur is to experience plush softness beyond measure.

Russian explorers discovered sea otters, and the value of their fur, while exploring Prince William Sound during the 1741 Bering Expedition. Word traveled as fast as the boats could sail, and soon Alaska had

OPPOSITE—*Two otters on an ice floe in Surprise Inlet, Harriman Fiord*

TOP—*Protected by their dense fur, a mother sea otter and pup float comfortably on their backs.*

BOTTOM—*Sea otters, the smallest marine mammals in North America, have gradually come back after thousands perished during the 1989 Exxon Valdez oil spill. There is now a stable population of about four thousand sea otters in Prince William Sound.*

a thriving commercial fur trade. During its heyday, Russians obtained and traded more than 175,000 otter pelts, with many sold in China where the fur was considered a sign of wealth.

When Alexander Walker explored the North west Coast to Alaska in 1785–86, he wrote in his journal that a sea otter pelt was worth five blue beads. Beads were of great value, particularly blue ones, for coastal Native people, who traded otter pelts for them. By the early 1900s, only two thousand otters remained in scattered pockets along the coast, a mere 1 percent of the estimated population before the fur trade.

We almost lost them. But, protected by the 1911 International Fur Seal Treaty, sea otters have gradually made a strong comeback with successful reintroduction efforts and further restrictions under the Marine Mammal Protection Act. The world population has grown to more than one hundred thousand. They are, however, still a threatened species within some stocks.

In Prince William Sound, sea otters have faced the challenge of a double recovery. After traders nearly exterminated them for their fur, humans accidently killed them with oil. Horrific images of oil-covered sea otters dying after the *Exxon Valdez* spill cannot be erased, nor should they be forgotten. An estimated three thousand sea otters perished from the oil, many from ingesting it as they groomed themselves to remove the goo. Some scratched their eyes out because they couldn't see. We sometimes forget that oil is a poison and that the stuff we put in our cars comes with environmental risk and cost, potentially lethal.

A lone sea otter sits atop a large,
blue iceberg in Columbia Bay.

But nature can be resilient, given time. In 2014, the *Exxon Valdez* Oil Spill Trustee Council reported that the sea otter was among the marine species that had fully recovered from the spill. A recent estimate reports a stable population of about four thousand sea otters in the Sound. It took a quarter of a century for the otters to recover from the toxic effects of oil in the environment.

Watching the mother sea otter wrap her forearms around the pup, I'm struck by the mother's humanlike cradling, grateful that we still have these animals on Earth, and hopeful that one day oil spills will be tragic events only found in history books.

A sea otter rests on ice in Barry Arm.

Aerial view of the face
of Columbia Glacier and
ice-choked Columbia
Bay, taken in 2008

LEFT—*The blue-grey waters of Columbia Bay are relatively ice free now; twenty years ago this area held two thousand feet of ice.*

OPPOSITE—*The massive face of the main branch of the Columbia Glacier*

LEFT—*Northern shovelers take flight in early spring from the edge of winter ice in Nassau Fiord.*

RIGHT—*Icebergs from the Columbia Glacier lay scattered around a small bay on the old terminal moraine.*

LEFT—*During the northern migration, surfbirds rest in the rocky intertidal zone on the moraine in Unakwik Inlet, located at Cannery Creek. These birds are bound for their nesting grounds in the alpine tundra habitat of the Alaska Range and Brooks Range.*

TOP—*A common loon hunts for small fish near the glacial moraine in Unakwik Inlet, located at Cannery Creek.*

The Great Temperate Rainforest

Staircase Meadows

My ears feel sunbaked on this glorious hot day in July. The Sound is calm and glassy, a bright metallic expanse studded with evergreen islands and peninsulas. In the distance, we spot the backlit blows of humpback whales. Sea otters lounge off the bow of the *Dora Keen*, then duck beneath the surface as we pass them.

Tim Lydon turns the boat to the north, the sun warming our backs. We're heading up Unakwik Inlet, not far from the old settlement of Kiniklik. The Kiniklik people were one of the eight Chugachmiut tribes whose traditional homeland extended from College Fiord to Valdez Arm. In 1925, during the heyday of gold and copper mining in the region, Kiniklik was abandoned. Introduced diseases such as tuberculosis and influenza took their toll on Native communities. Many villagers relocated to the larger

OPPOSITE—*Upland peat bog meadows filled with mountain hemlock and stunted bonsai Sitka spruce dot a granitic mountainside in Wells Bay.*

communities of Cordova and Valdez and found cannery jobs.

It is hard to imagine the bustling gold and copper mining activity, cannery facilities, and fox farms that existed on the Sound during the first half of the twentieth century. At one time, there were three active gold mines, sixteen fox farms (more about these later), and four salmon canneries in the region now designated the Nellie Juan–College Fiord Wilderness Study Area. All those operations are now part of Alaska's boom-and-bust history, which left behind toppled log cabins, rusty artifacts, and mossy tree stumps.

Prince William Sound is one of the few places in Alaska that has grown more wild over the past century since Klondike Gold Rush days.

Motoring up Wells Bay, we see no other boats or people. There's a quiet feeling of primitive wilderness with only the shrill whistle of a bald eagle to welcome us. Salmon dimple the bay, rising and breaking the surface. Harbor seals follow, their torpedo bodies chasing salmon beneath the boat. Pulses of pink salmon ripple toward the main inlet stream. The run is on.

Tim spots a black bear sow and cub near the shore, and fish carcasses litter the stream bank. As we approach, the bears duck for cover in the thick alders.

Tim explains, "Within a few steps of the shoreline, you have a mosaic of habitats. Glaciers and alpine tundra flirt with bog meadows, rainforest, and beach habitat."

Terraced meadows provide a perfect way to hike through the forest and reach higher elevations without bushwhacking. If we zigzag up the connecting meadows, we can reach alpine tundra and eventually scale three-thousand-foot granite ridges with distant views of the Columbia Glacier—all in the span of a few miles from the sea. Tim and Sebastian discuss the unusual nature of this staircase meadow environment.

Tim emphasizes that we are on the northern edge of the temperate rainforest and that this mosaic of

peat meadows and forest is unique. The interspersed mix of forest and open meadows is natural, not caused by clear-cutting as one might think at first glance. The patchwork of meadows offers great hiking and access to vistas. Sebastian suggests that we call the ascending meadows "stair meadows," a perfect descriptive term.

From the *Dora Keen* we plot an easy route through the forest. We can see the contours of the hills rising and falling above us as though someone had kneaded the earth, creating slopes and ravines for the forest, meadow pathways, and shrubby swales and squishy peat bogs. We see a gallery of rainforest trees: Sitka spruce, western hemlock, alder, mountain hemlock, and yellow cedar.

After anchoring the *Dora Keen* we row our dinghy to shore. Cautious, we carry bear spray. I'm anxious to explore this forest with Tim Lydon as guide, a person whose knowledge and passion for the wild Chugach National Forest are inspiring.

Final Stronghold for Yellow Cedars

As we ascend the stair meadows, Tim introduces me to one of the oldest yellow cedars near the northern extent of its range. Here trees struggle to grow on the fringe of the largest temperate rainforest in the world. This yellow cedar is only about forty feet tall, with a two-foot-diameter trunk, yet it might be seven hundred or more years old. As a young cedar, this one may have lived during times of the bubonic plague in Europe.

This beautiful tree has a delicious fragrance, a cross between mint and pine, subtle but sweet. Its weeping branches appear soft and fern-like, with layered fronds of feathery needles. The cedars have a conical shape that stands out amid the tall Sitka spruce and western hemlock trees.

OPPOSITE—*Alaska yellow cedars grow in the scattered stands of coastal temperate rainforest between stair meadows in Cedar Bay.*

In recent decades yellow cedars have suffered from climate change in more southerly locations, such as Southeast Alaska and British Columbia, where the snowfall is decreasing. Without insulating snow, their shallow roots freeze to death during winter. The cedars lose their needles and gradually wither away. These stressed and dying trees are now being considered for protection under the Endangered Species Act. The northern reaches of the Chugach National Forest may be the last stronghold for the yellow cedars, as long as there is protective winter snow.

We follow the stair meadows, gradually gaining elevation. Each meadow offers an open vista of Wells Bay, an intimate view of the landscape, and the ever-present chorus of hermit thrush, Pacific wren, song sparrow, and chestnut-backed chickadee. Some meadows have sparkling ponds, dark jewels fringed with the emerald green of deer cabbage, low-bush blueberries, crowberries, mosses, and white spongy lichens that look like miniature cauliflowers bubbling up from the meadow. The walking is soft, squishy, forgiving.

Stunted mountain hemlocks make me pause to study their distinctive shapes. Unlike the tall stands of western hemlock and Sitka spruce that crowd together, the squatty mountain hemlock is often alone. It is adapted to this soggy, spongy meadow environment. Sculptured by wind, rain, and snow, mountain hemlocks are gnarled and irregular, with twisted, curving branches. They seem to do Tai Chi, each with a unique pose. The enduring mountain hemlock can overcome obstacles of poorly drained soils, fierce winds, and heavy snows, living on the edge.

After a snack and lingering views, we descend toward the bay, listening to the soft warbling of pine grosbeaks. These beautiful finches live year-round in coastal evergreens, surviving on cone seeds that they pry open with their hefty beaks. One red-breasted grosbeak perches in a spruce tree with long wispy lichens dangling from the branches. These pale greenish lichens known as Methuselah's beard (*Usnea longissima*) can flourish in humid conditions near saltwater. Each strand can grow six feet long or more. These rootless plants are sensitive to air pollution and can serve as a good air quality indicator.

Forest Service workers collect a similar, more common species of lichen known as witch's hair (*Alectoria sarmentosa*) to monitor air pollution not only from cruise ships and motorboats but even from distant places such as China. On an earlier trip, I volunteered to help collect and bag these lichens with ecologist Kate Mohatt. The absorbent lichens provide a forensic signature that shows each pollutant and its source. Amazingly, scientists can identify and trace the journey of a carbon molecule from the smokestack of a cruise ship to a dangling lichen on a spruce tree. If you are a polluter, there is no way to hide.

As we leave Wells Bay, I reflect on this beautiful rainforest and the character of its trees and meadows. The purpose of our hike was to focus on the forest ecosystem, yet I long to come back and scale one of the three-thousand-foot peaks above Wells Bay. In just a four-mile ascent, a climber might get a magnificent view of the Columbia Glacier and the Chugach peaks rising above the sea. Someday.

Distant Island

We head southwest on the *Dora Keen* to several campsites and anchorage points near Icy Bay. As we follow Dangerous Passage, Tim watches for rocks, eyes focused on the nautical depth chart on an illuminated screen. Rocks show up as asterisks, and several places in the passage have veritable constellations.

Jackpot Bay, Gaanaak Cove, and Dual Head are stops along the way. At Dual Head, Tim runs the dinghy to the beach to check on the camp of a commercial guide from Wyoming. He enjoys meeting visitors to

OPPOSITE—*A fledgling Pacific wren perches in moss on the rainforest floor at Coghill Lake while waiting for its parent to deliver food.*

the Sound, hearing about their experiences, and helping them if needed. We talk with kayakers at Gaanaak Cove who have a beautiful campsite in a quiet spot. An eagle's nest is the only visible evidence that they have a neighbor.

Soon we reach Prince of Wales Passage as we head toward the southernmost point of the wilderness study area. This route is a new one for Tim, so there is excitement onboard. We see no other boats along this passage and feel like pioneers in a wilderness marine park. The mountains are shrouded with misty, dark green trees. Trees stacked upon trees, spilling into the sea.

Suddenly the passage widens, yawning toward the North Pacific. The sea breeze intensifies, the swells grow higher, and the *Dora Keen* seesaws. To the west we see Procession Rocks, black angular rocks that form a great natural signpost for sailors. A procession of murres escorts us, maybe one hundred or more strung out across the water like line dancers. We spot a few humpback whales blowing in the distance, their flukes rising as they sound. I sense a wild edginess to this place where the Sound meets the open sea. Somewhere out there is Hawaii, and somehow humpback whales know the way.

Soon we find a horseshoe-shaped cove, on the protected side of Elrington Island. We anchor the boat and row the dinghy to shore. On a narrow isthmus, we walk through a forest of young spruce and hemlock trees similar in size, diameter, and height. They likely have the same birthday, sprouting on land formerly submerged. We are close to the collision point where the Pacific Plate undercut and lifted the North American Plate, the monstrous jolt that heaved the marine world into daylight. The violent 1964 earthquake lifted Elrington Island twenty feet or more, creating a new shoreline. These trees took root on the shelf of freshly exposed land.

An older forest rises up behind this homogenized earthquake forest. Huge Sitka spruces loom above us,

draped with moss and wispy lichens. Some of these massive trees encase old moss-covered stumps, revealing the tree cutting of a fox farmer who lived here in 1919. A few scraps of tin roofing and several tree stumps are all that remain.

Fox farming in Prince William Sound dates to 1894 when a Swedish immigrant established the first fox farm on Seal Island. At the 1925 peak, thirty-four islands in Prince William Sound had fox farming operations. Islands were ideal spots for keeping the foxes contained. A farmer could rent an island from the Forest Service for twenty-five dollars a year. Many of the permit holders were tough sourdoughs who had arrived in Alaska before or during the Klondike Gold Rush in the last years of the nineteenth century.

The fox furs were shipped to places like St. Louis, where women preferred to wear silver or red fox. European women desired blue or arctic fox, and many of those furs were shipped to London and Paris.

The Valdez Dock Company exported approximately $100,000 worth of furs to Europe in 1922, as described in Jim and Nancy Lethcoe's *A History of Prince William Sound*. After the 1929 stock market crash, demand for furs declined, prices dropped, and the fox farms gradually closed.

On Elrington Island one hundred years ago, a lone fox farmer had no contact with the outside world. Transportation usually consisted of a dory and two oars. There was no radio communication. No marine weather forecasts. A fox farmer there was most isolated on the southern fringe of the Sound, with the open ocean lashing the outer coast of the island. The nearest settlement was Latouche, a small community next to the largest copper mine in the Sound. This meant twenty miles of rowing if one had an emergency or needed supplies.

The half-mile isthmus is a distinctive feature of Prince William Sound and the wilderness study area. In just ten minutes you can walk across the forested isthmus from calm, protected waters to the rough, outer coast, where breaking waves pound a crescent beach that is dappled with orange and purple rocks. These unusual stones have high concentrations of oxidized iron and magnesium as found in seafloor volcanic rocks. That seafloor has gradually uplifted over millions of years to its present location. From this colorful beach you can see forever across the boundless North Pacific.

The narrow isthmus connects two kidney-shaped land formations that jut into the sea. These two lobes face each other, rising steeply above the water, with the isthmus bridging them. On a map this looks like a set of headphones, and the formation actually does create a unique stereophonic soundscape. Back on the *Dora Keen*, drifting in this amphitheater, we experience nature's surround sound. Each breaking wave, cry of gull, song of hermit thrush, and breath of whale is amplified, with a richness and resonance that makes you pause and listen.

HUMMINGBIRDS FROM AFAR

Perched on a hill above a small harbor, Chenega Bay is a small fishing village on Evans Island. After docking the *Dora Keen*, we walk through the community, past brightly colored houses that line a quiet dirt road. It appears that many residents are out fishing on this brilliant, sunny day.

Chenega Bay is a relatively new Chugachmiut village, established in the 1980s in a resettlement effort. The historic village of Chenega on nearby Chenega Island was destroyed by the massive tsunami from the 1964 earthquake, and a third of the village residents lost their lives. Surviving families and others worked together to build this new community, which is surrounded by the Chugach National Forest and the wilderness study area.

Kate McLaughlin greets us in the middle of the road, anxious to share news about the many rufous hummingbirds that migrate to her backyard each spring. Living in Chenega Bay, Kate, a biologist and environmental consultant, has developed a passion for and deep interest in these delicate creatures that magically arrive at her feeder from distant lands. She began studying them in 2007 and gradually became a licensed hummingbird bander, one of about a hundred specialized banders in the United States.

Kate now runs the northernmost hummingbird banding station in America. In 2010, she recaptured one banded rufous hummingbird from Tallahassee, Florida. This set a new migration record—a distance of more than thirty-five hundred miles, the world's longest documented migration of any hummingbird. And this bird weighs just a bit more than a penny.

Kate cares profoundly about the well-being of Prince William Sound. In addition to monitoring the northernmost-breeding hummingbird in

the world, she is president and director of Prince William Soundkeeper, a grassroots advocacy organization that works to preserve the water quality of the Sound through stewardship, advocacy, and education. In response to the *Exxon Valdez* oil spill, this group has diligently worked to keep waters and beaches pristine and to prevent such accidents from ever happening again.

Outside her window is a hummingbird feeder surrounded by a trapdoor cage. Kate spots a juvenile rufous hummingbird zooming into the enclosure. She closes the gate using a remote control gadget, then hurries outside to catch the tiny bird in a mesh bag. She carefully brings the bird inside and places it in a nylon sock to keep it calm and still.

As she prepares to band the bird, the green iridescent wisp of life clings to a toothpick with its minuscule toes. Calm and focused, Kate measures and weighs it, then places a hair-thin band on its leg—a band one-sixteenth by one-quarter inch long. The bird plays dead during this process, seemingly relaxed on the dining room table. Kate is a pro.

Before Kate started the Alaska Hummingbird Project she had no idea how many hummingbirds visited her feeder each summer. Now she knows, having captured as many as five hundred individuals in one summer. Some of her banded birds have been recaptured during the winter in places such as Steamboat Springs, Colorado; Mill Valley, California; and Fort Davis, Texas.

Why would such a tiny, lightweight bird fly so far north? Rufous hummingbirds thrive on nectar, and Alaska has a profusion of summer blossoms from wildflowers and berry bushes. In particular, they are attracted to red, tubular flowers such as columbine. They also eat

Biologist Kate McLaughlin checks on a hummingbird feeder near her home in Chenega Bay. (Debbie Miller)

protein-rich insects and spiders that are usually plentiful. With the long summer days in Alaska, these hummingbirds can feed nearly round the clock during their breeding season, an added advantage for nurturing their young.

Evidently the word is out that Kate's feeder is regularly replenished. Scores of these flying jewels continue to return to her home beginning in late April. Many of the birds have a strong fidelity to their winter and summer homes, returning to the same flowering bushes and breeding location. There is a chance that the Tallahassee hummingbird hatched in a lichen-covered nest woven with strands of spider web, not far from Kate's home on this far-flung island.

OPPOSITE LEFT—"*Chicken of the woods,*" *a colorful and edible fungus, grows on the trunk of a western hemlock in the rainforest located in upper Cedar Bay.*

OPPOSITE RIGHT—*A rufous hummingbird feeds on highbush blueberry blossoms.*

RIGHT—*Wells Bay and Cedar Bay are the only two places in northern Prince William Sound where Alaska yellow cedar grows.*

TOP—*A varied thrush searches for beach fleas during low tide in McClure Bay, Port Nellie Juan.*

BOTTOM—*During spring migration, an American robin looks for food in storm-tossed seaweed and eel grass on Glacier Island.*

TOP—Chestnut-backed chickadees are year-round residents in the spruce and hemlock forests of the WSA. This chickadee paused for a moment in early spring while searching for food to bring back to its nest located in a cavity in a dead hemlock near Coghill Lake.

BOTTOM—White-winged crossbills rely on the seeds of spruce and tamarack trees as their primary source of food.

LEFT—*The glacier-melt fed Cascade Waterfall, the largest waterfall in Prince William Sound, pours out of the mountains between College Fiord and Eaglek Bay, into Cascade Bay.*

OPPOSITE LEFT—*Remnants of the hydropower plant that supplied electricity to a salmon cannery in Sawmill Bay and was destroyed in the 1964 earthquake*

OPPOSITE RIGHT—*An old ore cart is being slowly taken over by the rainforest at the Culross Gold Mine on Culross Island.*

Loss
and Hope

Tracing the Past

Barbara Lydon steers the *Dora Keen* around the northern tip of Eleanor Island, carefully avoiding volcanic outcroppings composed of pillow basalts. These spherical rocks look like soft gray pillows piled on top of each other. Eva Saulitis, who spent much of her life studying orcas in these waters, described them as "gnomish lobes of rock"—formations that were created millions of years ago, when oozing magma bubbled up from the seafloor and cooled quickly.

Eleanor Island is on the northern fringe of a spectacular cluster of islands known as the Knight Island complex. On Knight Island itself, dark mountains and ridges rise steeply to twenty-five hundred feet above the water. Three prominent peaks have a chiseled, angular appearance that reminds me of the Grand Tetons. They are part of a magnificent rampart that separates Knight Island Passage from Montague Strait.

Barbara searches for a sheltered cove to drop anchor. A bright bundle of energy, she is incredibly skilled at piloting the *Dora Keen*. Fit and trim at five foot four, she is licensed to drive boats up to twenty-five tons with unlimited passengers. We are in good hands.

Forest Service archaeologist Heather Hall helps drop anchor while my daughter, Robin, and I stack gear in the stern of the boat. The four of us are on a work trip cleaning up beaches, checking campsites,

OPPOSITE—*Pillow basalts in submarine volcanic rocks are exposed near the entrance into Copper Bay on Knight Island—a partial "ophiolite" or uplifted exposed slab of oceanic crust.*

and investigating archaeology sites. Soon Robin and I are setting up her new "leave no trace" aerial tent. Cinched tightly to three anchor trees, the triangular tent hangs about four feet off the ground, providing a snug, rainproof shelter for us and our gear. This tent clearly leaves no impact on the land.

At thirty years old, Robin can easily spring off the forest floor and has enough strength to pull herself up. I, on the other hand, feel like a flailing child trying to do her first chin-up. Barbara mercifully gives me a boost.

Robin and I sleep like twin embryos in a womb, cradled by giant Sitka spruce. In the morning we dangle our legs out and drop to the ground, both of us feeling loose and flexible, as though we've just finished a yoga session. A new sleep experience!

This morning Heather guides me through a thick understory of ferns, blueberry bushes, and shrubby alders. Everything is lush, green, and wet. The elaborate trilling of a Pacific wren and the ethereal song of the varied thrush drift through the forest canopy. Heather points to a distinct scar on a tall hemlock, a vertical cut about six feet long and five inches wide. The tree looks healthy and strong.

Heather explains that the scarred hemlock is a good example of a culturally modified tree. The Chugachmiut people traditionally built rectangular plank houses constructed with long slabs of hemlock bark. They also harvested the cambium layer beneath the bark for food and other uses. Removing narrow vertical strips allowed the tree to keep growing, unlike girdled bark cuttings that would strangle the tree. There are hundreds of trees with plank cuttings around the Sound, showing centuries of sustainable human use.

In a plank house long ago, a woman would sit by an open hearth, roasting salmon or seal meat. A *tanqik*, or stone lamp, filled with seal oil and a burning wick of native cotton grass, would provide light and a bit of warmth. Blankets made from mountain goat, bear, or feathered cormorant skins might be found in the sleeping room. Seal gut skin stretched across an opening in the wall would serve as a translucent window.

The Chugachmiut diet was, and still is, rich and diverse, governed by the seasons. Kenny Selanoff, a subsistence hunter who grew up in Old Chenega before the 1964 earthquake, writes in *We Are the Land, We Are the Sea*: "Growing up, my family lived off the land. We ate seal, clam, duck, salmon, herring, *uuqiituks* [the shellfish known as gumboot chiton], sea cucumber, halibut, grouse, bear, and black seaweed. . . . You know how Popeye likes his spinach? That's how much I like my Native food."

The culture of Chugachmiut people is bonded deeply to their homeland. How tragic that two of the most catastrophic events in American history brought immeasurable losses to the Chugachmiut communities. First, the devastating tsunami from the 1964 earthquake washed away Old Chenega and killed a third of its residents. Then, twenty-five years later, almost to the day, the *Exxon Valdez* spilled eleven million gallons of oil into Prince William Sound, poisoning their homeland and foods. Their fishing and gathering livelihood was compromised or destroyed. The herring population crashed and has yet to recover. Perhaps worst of all, their sacred burial sites were looted during the oil spill cleanup. They have endured such pain and loss.

Barbara and I dig into the wet sand and pebble beach, looking for signs of oil. A few feet down the water appears filmy, and we wonder if it is tainted. In 1989 the beaches of Eleanor Island and other surrounding islands were smothered with oil. During that tragic time and the months of cleanup that followed, countless television news reports showed birds and sea otters coated with sticky black crude. We saw the horror of what oil can do to a rich, beautiful world, and we painfully remember the loss of life.

One evening during the spill, Robin, then a two-year-old, sat at the dinner table as we watched the grim news. When she saw a person carrying a sea otter saturated with black goo, she started to cry. Sniffling, she said something I will never forget: "Mommy, when will the oil spill be over?"

Nearly thirty years have passed since the oil spill disaster. That same child now explores a beach once sheathed in black goo. She kneels down by a small tide pool, gazing into the water.

"Look at this beautiful anemone," she says, pointing, wide-eyed about her discovery.

Green tentacles dancing, the anemone looks healthy in its cradle of sparking water. Nature is resilient, but it can sometimes take decades. It's estimated that about sixty-one tons of trapped oil still remain beneath the sand in many tidal areas harmed by the spill. The wilderness around Prince William Sound looks clean and pristine on the surface, but unseen harm still persists on the fringe of that wilderness.

Looking across the Sound, I see Hinchinbrook Island, known as Nuchek or Nuuciq, to the Chugachmiut people. In earlier times, the largest Native settlement in Prince William Sound was located on this island, as was a Russian trading post. Today the Chugach Heritage Foundation runs the Nuuciq, Spirit Camp on the island, a summer program that teaches children the importance of their culture, language, and subsistence way of life.

The Nuuciq Spirit Camp builds hope for the future during this prolonged time of healing in Prince William Sound. May the Chugachmiut people continue to find strength and resilience for a bright and healthy future, sustaining their way of life and spirit in the years to come.

Names Tell Stories

For thousands of years, the Chugachmiut people have lived around Prince William Sound, fishing the waters, collecting mussels and clams, hunting for sea otters and sea lions, and harvesting berries and other edible plants. These Indigenous people have hundreds of place names that describe the landscape, waters, cultural resources, and stories about geographic locations. Such names are meaningful to the culture, descriptive and respectful of the surroundings, with no intent to convey ownership as so many Euro-American names do. Today, very few of these names show up on maps.

When European explorers arrived in the eighteenth century, the protocol for naming places was largely chauvinistic, with little regard for the physical features of the landscape or stories that reflected human interaction with that landscape. Explorers often named places after sponsors of their expedition, distant institutions, or royal family members whom they served. These names fill our maps today, masking Indigenous cultures.

Take, for example, *Prince William Sound*. When Captain James Cook dropped anchor here in 1778, he decided to name this expansive body of sheltered water Sandwich Sound, after his patron, John Montagu, Earl of Sandwich. He also named the two islands that shielded the Sound: Montague Island, the largest uninhabited island in America, and the smaller Hinchinbrook Island, after Montagu's father, Viscount Hinchinbrook.

Montagu was said to have been a busy man who liked to eat quick meals by slapping a piece of meat

THE ORIGIN OF "CHUGACH"

Oral tradition records describe how the Native name *Chugach* came to be. This story was shared by the late John Klashinoff, who was born in the village of Nuchek, in Prince William Sound, in 1906.

"For ages and ages Prince William Sound, as it was named by Captain James Cook, was covered by a solid sheet of glacier ice that extended over nearly all of the bays and mountains. One day Native hunters were kayaking along the outer shores of the Pacific Ocean, when a man cried out:

"*Chu-ga, chu-ga*"—"Hurry, hurry."

"Let's go see what that black thing is sticking out of the ice."

So the hunters paddled closer and closer to see what it was. Within a short distance, the hunters could see mountaintops emerging out of the retreating ice. Thus these ocean travelers settled along the ice-free shores of the Sound.

As the seasons changed from year to year, the ice melted rapidly, exposing deep fjords and lagoons that were rich in sea life and provided good beaches to settle on. It was known that life thrived in the areas where the salt and fresh water met.

When the ice retreated, so did the animals. The Chugach people followed the ice and animals deep into the heart of Prince William Sound, where they remain to this very day."

known to the Chugachmiut people as *Nuuciq*, meaning "last land before the open water." Long before Captain Cook arrived, the largest uninhabited island that shields the Sound was known as *Tsuklak*, meaning "terrible island," perhaps because it is difficult ot land a boat on the island's east side. These original names pertain directly to the geography, not to people who never set foot in Alaska.

Some other descriptive names around the Sound:

Eshamy Bay: from the Alutiiq word *Is'ami*, modified from the Eyak word *ishxah*, meaning "basket"; also possibly means "good fishing place"

Guguak Bay: possibly derived from the Alutiiq *Kugya'ik*, meaning "small place for setting nets"

Chenega: "below the mountain"

Gaanaak Cove: from the Alutiiq word *Yaamaak* or *Gaamaak*, meaning "two rocks"

Ek'agutak Bay: derived from the Alutiiq word *Ek'aqataq*, meaning "going across"

The original names of thousands of places around Prince William Sound have faded to a whisper. We can hope, however, that more of these evocative and meaningful names may someday be returned to their rightful places on maps.

between two slices of bread, the supposed origin of the word *sandwich* as we know it today. Cartographers later changed the name from *Sandwich Sound* to *Prince William Sound* to honor the prince who later became Britain's King William IV, known to some as Silly Billy.

The Chugachmiut people once referred to the Sound as Chugach Bay, and the meaning of the word *Chugach* is explained through John F. E. Johnson's story, as passed down to him by his ancestors (see sidebar). For centuries, Hinchinbrook Island has been

Disappearing Orcas

On a rocky beach, I gaze across the Sound toward the Pleiades, a distinct group of islands named after the star cluster said to represent the Seven Sisters of Greek mythology. The string of islands runs north–south like a compass needle. Glassing the water toward Icy Bay, I look for orcas, or killer whales, but see none this day.

This is the place where biologist and writer Eva Saulitis studied her beloved, genetically distinct pod of transient orcas over the course of twenty-five years.

Her book *Into Great Silence: A Memoir of Discovery and Loss Among Vanishing Orcas* is perhaps the finest tribute to these magnificent creatures ever written. A few years after her book was published, Eva succumbed to cancer at age fifty-three, a great loss that echoes her story of the Chugach transients.

Eva came to know the Chugach transient orcas by listening to their vocalizations and by carefully watching their behaviors as she followed their movements in Prince William Sound with her partner, Craig Matkin. Unlike the less mobile "resident orcas" that are fish eaters, "transients" roam widely, hunting for seals and other marine mammals. Their movements are less predictable in their stealthy quest to surprise their prey.

When Eva began her studies before the *Exxon Valdez* oil spill, there were twenty-two members in the pod, each identified by sex, age, and voice and given a descriptive name such as Eyak, Eccles, Egagutak, Ewan, Ripple Fin, Mike, Chenega, and Iktua. Some traveled together in familiar small groups, and Eva came to know and love them as friends—their personalities and hunting skills, their silences and outbursts, their acrobatics and songs, and eventually their disappearances. The *Exxon Valdez* oil spill killed or poisoned most of the Chugach transient orcas. No calves have been born since the 1989 spill, and only seven members remain, with no females able to bear young. Their distinct genetic population will inevitably become extinct, along with the unique dialect that only the Chugach transients speak.

Today Chenega, Iktua, Mike, Marie, Ewan, Paddy, and Egagutak are the last survivors of a group whose ancestors probably lived in Prince William Sound for thousands of years. Theirs is a heartbreaking story of what happens when massive amounts of oil are spilled into a vibrant and diverse community. If ever we need reminding of the need to move toward a clean energy future, to break from our addiction to oil, and to actively address climate change, let us remember the Chugach orcas.

KEEPING THE SOUND PRISTINE

With callused hands, bronze face, and toned muscles, he wears a dirty T-shirt and smiles. Scott Groves is a tall man of iron who lifts every day, but not at the gym. He's just returned from a month of cleaning up trash on the beaches of Montague Island. Montague and Hinchin-brook Island form a long shield protecting Prince William Sound and the beaches of the wilderness study area from the rough outer waters of the Gulf of Alaska.

These barrier islands are situated ideally to receive ocean debris that has drifted from as far away as Japan. Near the convergence of the North Pacific and Gulf of Alaska gyres, floating trash swirls toward the long outer coast of Montague, where drifting logs are thrown up like toothpicks on beaches during a big storm, with monstrous swells as high as thirty to forty feet and gale-force winds.

Scott describes the impressive work of the Gulf of Alaska Keeper organization: "On Montague Island we pick up twenty to thirty tons of garbage per mile of beach on average." Since its formation in 2005, Gulf of Alaska Keeper has removed more than three million pounds of toxic plastic debris from over fifteen hundred miles of beaches. It is the leading organization in North America for collecting marine debris.

Each summer Scott and crew clean up countless plastic items, buoys, Styrofoam, and thousands of remnant rubber mats full of cutouts from manufactured flip-flop soles. In recent years as much as half of the marine debris stemmed from Japan's 2011 tsunami. Fishing nets are the worst. On one work trip it took four days to extract a six-thousand-pound trawling net that was entangled and partially buried on the shore.

At an average rate of a quarter mile per day, Scott and his team have combed, collected, and bagged many miles of beach debris, and each year Gulf of Alaska Keeper hauls out enough bags to fill a barge.

Scott loves his work and looks forward to more of it. "I like seeing the progress of changing the environment, making it more pristine. I get to work for a fantastic organization and spend time in one of the most beautiful places in the world."

OPPOSITE—As returning sunlight brings an explosion of life to Prince William Sound in spring, a humpback whale shows its flukes as it begins a deep feeding dive, Unakwik Inlet.

Scott Groves (Sarah Mastroyanis)

LEFT—*A "smack" of moon jellies congregates for sexual reproduction in Eaglek Bay.*

OPPOSITE TOP—*Anemones exposed by low tide, cover the rocks in the tidal chuck, or channel, that connects a large tidal lagoon in Schoppe Bay to Eaglek Bay. Large amounts of water rush through the chuck at every tidal change bringing abundant food to these filter feeders.*

OPPOSITE BOTTOM—*Prince William Sound spot prawns (actually a shrimp) harvested by commercial fishermen in College Fiord*

OPPOSITE RIGHT—*Elderberry bushes produce abundant red berry clusters at the edge of the rainforest environment in upper Cedar Bay.*

Epilogue

A Promise of Wilderness

Many years ago, a couple from New York made a promise to each other. They dreamed of visiting Alaska and seeing its magnificent wilderness. Lee and Barb would save up for the special trip they would make someday.

During years of anticipation, Lee had his doubts. He did not believe that true wilderness really existed. He had never seen it.

Now, onboard the *Discovery*, Lee sits next to me, and his eyes glisten with tears. He is astonished and moved by his experience in Prince William Sound and seeing the Nellie Juan–College Fiord Wilderness Study Area. An elderly man, Lee relaxes in an armchair and reflects on the untouched beauty, the spectacular glaciers and mountains, the pristine streams crowded with salmon, the moss-cloaked rainforest. He is stunned by the realization that such a wild place does still exist.

Shaking his head, Lee softly reflects, "This is *real* wilderness."

Alaska is blessed with some of the wildest and most beautiful wilderness remaining on our planet. Just say the word *Alaska* to people you meet, from anywhere, and they will light up with keen interest, even excitement. Alaska's greatest resource is its wilderness. Long after the gold and oil are gone, it will be Alaska's wild that sustains and nourishes its people and visitors from around the world—if we are good stewards and do all we can to protect it.

While some of Alaska's wilderness is now protected in national parks, wildlife refuges, and forests, the Chugach National Forest, with some of the most dramatic and spectacular land in the world, has not one acre of designated wilderness. The Nellie Juan–College Fiord Wilderness Study Area could easily be degraded by mining, other development, and increased public use. Congress has ignored past wilderness proposals for this area, even though it has been recognized as a wilderness study area for nearly four decades.

The wilderness that embraces Prince William Sound is Alaska at its dazzling best. Will Congress permanently protect this stunningly beautiful place so that the greater promise of wilderness can be fulfilled for all people, for every future generation, and for the sake of leaving this precious piece of the planet in its unaltered state?

Now is the time for all of us to raise our voices and ask the Forest Service and Congress to take action. This extraordinary mosaic of mountains, ice fields, waterfalls, glaciers, rainforest, meadows, rivers, and estuaries—and the kaleidoscopic array of life within—is worthy of full protection through a wilderness designation. We offer this book toward that goal.

OPPOSITE—*A sea otter pup clings to its mother as she paddles through thick ice in Surprise Inlet, Harriman Fiord.*

Author Acknowledgments

I'm incredibly grateful that photographer and naturalist Hugh Rose invited me to collaborate on this book five years ago. Hugh brought to the project his passion, knowledge, and concern for protecting the wilderness around Prince William Sound. My profound thanks for his many years of work capturing the beautiful images in this book. It has been a great privilege to work with him.

Without the generous support of Dean Rand of Discovery Voyages, this book would not exist. Thank you, Dean, for guiding me on several *Discovery* trips, beginning in 2013. On each fantastic voyage, we explored the fjords, bays, forest, meadows, and the dynamic world of tidewater glaciers. There was always the element of excitement and surprise and the promise of wildlife encounters. What more could a writer hope for? Many, many thanks to Dean for being the best skipper ever and for sponsoring this book project.

I'm deeply grateful for the support of Tim and Barbara Lydon, wilderness stewards for the Chugach National Forest. It was an honor to be an artist-in-residence for the Forest Service and to explore the world of Prince William Sound with Tim and Barbara. Their work as dedicated stewards for the Nellie Juan–College Fiord Wilderness Study Area is exemplary. I tremendously appreciated the opportunities to travel through the Sound with Tim and Barbara and to learn about this magical place through their eyes.

A huge thanks to Richard Nelson for kayaking with me in College and Harriman fjords. I couldn't ask for a better adventure partner, paddler, and friend. I'm also indebted to Nels for carefully reviewing the manuscript, offering sage advice, making countless good suggestions, and offering positive encouragement throughout the writing process.

Many wonderful people kindly shared their knowledge, reviewed sections of the manuscript, answered questions, provided references, and gave editorial feedback: Tim and Barbara Lydon, Dean and Heather Rand, Hugh Rose, Shad O'Neel, Kate Mohatt, Kate McLaughlin, Heather Hall, Michelle Koppes, Jenna Cragg, Craig Matkin, Michelle Kissling, Kathy Kuletz, Matthew O'Leary, Daniel Esler, John Pearce, Lori Chase, Dagmar Etkin, Robin Miller, Casey Miller, Bob Hume, Peg Faithful, Scott Groves, and Dave Sczawinski, and Helen Woods with the *Exxon Valdez* Oil Spill Trustee Council.

Thanks to John F. E. Johnson for sharing his knowledge and heritage, for reviewing the manuscript, and for giving permission to publish the Chugach origin story passed down to him from his Chugachmiut ancestors.

A special thanks to Mike Wurtz, head of Special Collections, University Library, University of the Pacific, in Stockton, California. He kindly allowed me to review John Muir's original journals from the 1899 Harriman Alaska Expedition. What a treasured moment to see Muir's *original* penciled words and drawings of Prince William Sound. Some of Muir's sketches from the expedition are included in this book by permission of the Holt-Atherton Center for Western Studies.

Last, I feel honored and thankful to work with publisher Helen Cherullo at Braided River and the team of editors and designers whose collaborative efforts created this book. Braided River cares deeply about protecting wild places in Alaska and the Pacific Northwest, places such as the wilderness that surrounds Prince William Sound. For this I am deeply and humbly grateful.

Photographer Acknowledgments

I am deeply grateful to Dean Rand, captain and owner of the M/V *Discovery*. After a mutual friend introduced us twenty years ago, Dean exposed me to the wilderness of Prince William Sound on board the *Discovery* and got me hooked on the place. That initial trip marked the beginning of a long friendship that has included me working on the *Discovery* and being transported into the stunning beauty of the Nellie Juan–College Fiord area to photograph and explore for many weeks every summer since! As a naturalist working for Dean, I have helped introduce our passengers to the breathtaking landscape of Prince William Sound, interpreting what they see, and then motivating them to be voices for wilderness preservation. Without Dean's generous financial support of this project, this book would not have come to fruition; for this I will be forever grateful.

My profound thanks go to author and wilderness advocate, Debbie Miller. Without Debbie's encouragement and inspiring writing this book wouldn't have a voice. Debbie's descriptive and evocative prose gives a narrative to my photos that weaves them together into a cohesive story they otherwise would have been lacking.

My original introduction to Dean was through our great mutual friend Patrick Endres, an Alaskan photographer who has been an inspiration to me in my career as an outdoor/nature photographer since we first met in Denali Park twenty-five years ago. Thank you, Patrick.

Steve Raney and his mother, Gayle Raney, have both been inspirational to me. Staying at Steve's lodge in Cordova (Orca Adventure Lodge) and flying around the Sound with Gayle and Steve provided many wonderful photo opportunities. Steve made time in his busy summer schedule to make sure I was in the air on the ideal day for capturing the aerial glacier images and precisely piloted the plane for the perfect positions!

Thank you to all the wonderful people I have met and learned so much from in Prince William Sound over the years. Oyster Dave (Dave Sczawinski), Gordon Scott, Tim and Barbara Lydon, and all the crew members whom I have worked with on the *Discovery* over the years including Dean Rand's daughters, Heather and Hannah, and Andy and Seawan Craig.

I am deeply grateful for the WSA because it's where I met my partner of the last fourteen years, Ali Blechman. She has been insightful and supportive throughout this project.

A heartfelt thank you to all the participants of the Braided River book benefit cruises on board the M/V *Discovery* in May of 2016 and 2017. Your discussions about Prince William Sound and the wilderness were inspiring.

And last, I am honored to have worked with Helen Cherullo and her team at Braided River to bring this collection of photographs and Debbie's writing together into a cohesive narrative that so eloquently tells the story of the Nellie Juan–College Fiord Wilderness Study Area. I remember when Helen changed her travel plans at the last minute to stay an extra week in Alaska to join a trip on the *Discovery* and see the WSA for the first time, and the look in her eyes when she first saw College Fiord and came under the spell of that magical piece of Chugach National Forest. Thank you for your dedication to preserving wild places.

Bibliography

Arimitsu, Mayumi L., John F. Piatt, Erica N. Madison, Jeffrey S. Conaway, and Nicola Hillgruber. "Oceanographic Gradients and Seabird Prey Community Dynamics in Glacial Fjords." *Fisheries Oceanography* 21, nos. 2–3 (2012): 148–69.

Burroughs, John, John Muir, and George Bird Grinnell. *Alaska: Giving the Results of the Harriman Expedition*, vol. 1, *Narrative, Glaciers, Natives*. London: John Murray, 1902.

Chu, Jennifer. "Artificial Whisker Reveals Source of Harbor Seal's Uncanny Prey-Sensing Ability." MIT News, October 15, 2015. www.news.mit.edu/.

Crowell, Aron, Amy Steffian, and Gordon Pullar, eds. *Looking Both Ways: Heritage and Identity of the Alutiiq People*. Fairbanks, AK: University of Alaska Press, 2001.

Day, Angela. *Red Light to Starboard: Recalling the* Exxon Valdez *Disaster*. Pullman, WA: Washington State University Press, 2014.

Day, Robert H., A. Prichard, and D. Nigro. "Ecological Specialization and Overlap of Brachyramphus Murrelets in Prince William Sound." *Auk* 120, no. 3 (July 2003): 680–99.

Exxon Valdez Oil Spill Trustee Council. *Exxon Valdez Oil Spill Restoration Plan: 2014 Update for Injured Resources and Services*. Anchorage, AK: *Exxon Valdez* Oil Spill Trustee Council, 2014. www.evostc.state.ak.us/static/PDFs/2014IRSUpdate.pdf.

Felis, Jonathan J., Michelle L. Kissling, Robb S. A. Kaler, Leah A. Kenney, and Matthew J. Lawonn. "Identifying Kittlitz's Murrelet Nesting Habitat in North America at the Landscape Scale." *Journal of Fish and Wildlife Management* 7, no. 2 (2016): 323–33.

Frost, O. W., editor. "Nuchek." In *Bering and Chirikov: The American Voyages and Their Impact*. Anchorage, AK: Alaska Historical Society, 1992.

Gulick, Amy. *Salmon in the Trees: Life in Alaska's Tongass Rain Forest*. Seattle: Braided River, 2010.

Holleman, Marybeth. *Alaska's Prince William Sound: A Traveler's Guide*. Portland, OR: Alaska Northwest Books, 2000.

Johnson, John F. E. *Chugach Legends and Photographs of the Chugach Region*. Anchorage, AK: Chugach Alaska Corporation, 1984.

Kissling, Michelle L., Scott M. Gende, Stephen B. Lewis, and Paul M. Lukacs. "Reproductive Performance of Kittlitz's Murrelet in a Glaciated Landscape, Icy Bay, Alaska, USA." *Condor* 117, no. 2 (2015): 237–48.

Lethcoe, Jim. *An Observer's Guide to the Geology of Prince William Sound*. Valdez, AK: Prince William Sound Books, 1990.

Lethcoe, Jim, and Nancy Lethcoe. *A History of Prince William Sound Alaska*. Valdez, AK: Prince William Sound Books, 2001.

Matkin, Craig. *An Observer's Guide to the Killer Whales of Prince William Sound*. Valdez, AK: Prince William Sound Books, 1994.

McLaughlin, Kate. "Alaska's Amazing Rufous Hummingbird." *BirdWatching*, August 9, 2013. www.BirdWatchingDaily.com/.

Michelson, Pete. *Natural History of Prince William Sound*. Cordova, AK: Alaska Wild Wings, 1989.

Muir, John. Muir Papers, Journals 58, 59, 60, "Harriman Expedition to Alaska, 1899." Holt-Atherton Center for Western Studies, University of Pacific, Stockton, California.

Nelson, Richard K. *Make Prayers to the Raven*. Chicago: University of Chicago Press, 1983.

O'Neel, Shad, and Eran Hood. "Icefield-to-Ocean Linkages across the Northern Pacific Coastal Temperate Rainforest Ecosystem." *BioScience* 65, no. 5 (2015): 499–512.

Post, Anne. "Why Fish Need Trees and Trees Need Fish." *Alaska Fish and Wildlife News*, November 2008. www.adfg.alaska.gov/.

Post, Austin. *Preliminary Hydrography and Historic Terminal Changes of Columbia Glacier, Alaska*. Hydrological Investigations Atlas 559. Reston, VA: US Geological Survey, 1975.

Ruth, Maria Mudd. *Rare Bird: Pursuing the Mystery of the Marbled Murrelet*. Seattle: Mountaineers Books, 2013.

Saulitis, Eva. *Into Great Silence: A Memoir of Discovery and Loss among Vanishing Orcas*. Boston: Beacon Press, 2014.

Selanoff, Kenny. "A Lesson Learned." In *We Are the Land, We Are the Sea.*, ed. John E. Smelcer and Morgen A. Young, 95–97. Anchorage, AK: Chenega Heritage, 2007.

Steller, Georg Wilhelm. *Journal of a Voyage with Bering, 1741–1742*. Edited by O. W. Frost. Palo Alto: Stanford University Press, 1988.
———. *De Bestiis Marinis*. US: Zea E-Books, 2001

Van Blaricom, Glenn. *Sea Otters*. Stillwater, MN: Voyageur Press, 2001.

Viereck, Leslie A., and Elbert L. Little Jr. *Alaska Trees and Shrubs*. Fairbanks, AK: University of Alaska Press, 2007.

Voiland, Adam P. "Rapid Retreat." NASA Visualization Explorer, June 14, 2102. http://svs.gsfc.nasa.gov/10982.

Walker, Alexander. *An Account of a Voyage to the Northwest Coast of North America, 1785–1786*. Edited by R. A. Fisher and J. M. Bumsted. Seattle: University of Washington Press, 1982.

WITH APPRECIATION

To Captain Dean Rand of the *Discovery*, whose generosity and love of Prince William Sound made this book possible.

The *Discovery* is a classic sixty-five-foot working yacht built in 1958. A fourth-generation Presbyterian mission vessel, it once provided service as a vital link between small coastal Native Alaskan villages and the rest of the world. Today, Discovery Voyages offers intimate cruises in Alaska's Prince William Sound as a way to bring awareness to this vital, beautiful, and vulnerable ecosystem.

LEFT—*The* Discovery, *heading for a close encounter with Cascade Glacier*

TOP RIGHT—*Participants on the May 2016 M/V* Discovery *cruise that helped to fund the production of this book, out on a skiff tour of Nellie Juan Lagoon, with the Nellie Juan Glacier towering behind*

BOTTOM RIGHT—*Captain of the* Discovery, *Dean Rand*

ABOUT THE AUTHOR

A lover of wild places, Debbie Miller has explored and written about Alaska's wilderness and wildlife for more than four decades. She is the author of *Midnight Wilderness: Journeys in Alaska's Arctic National Wildlife Refuge* (Braided River) and numerous award-winning children's nature books about Alaska. She recently collaborated with photographer Hugh Rose and others to create *On Arctic Ground*, the first photo-essay book about the remote wilderness in the National Petroleum Reserve-Alaska.

Upon completion of those Arctic projects, Debbie and Hugh embarked on a journey to create a book about the magnificent coastal wilderness that surrounds Prince William Sound. As the 2014 artist-in-residence for the Chugach National Forest, Debbie began exploring and writing about America's largest wilderness study area. With a goal of designating this extraordinary place as wilderness, Debbie hopes that *A Wild Promise* will inspire readers to advocate for lasting protection of this unique landscape and its wildlife. To learn more about Debbie's work and life in Alaska visit www.debbiemilleralaska.com, or visit her on Facebook at www.facebook.com/debbiemilleralaska.

ABOUT THE PHOTOGRAPHER

Inspired by the rejuvenating nature of Alaska's wilderness, Hugh Rose has spent the last twenty-five years exploring and photographing its unparalleled natural beauty, wildlife, birds, plants, geology, and solitude from his base in Fairbanks. After graduate school and a brief career in geology, Hugh went north to work as a freelance photographer and a naturalist-guide in Denali, eventually focusing his guiding and photography on the Arctic and Prince William Sound. His goal in natural history interpretation and photography has been to show visitors to Alaska some of the last great wildernesses, while at the same time instilling a wilderness preservation ethic in them. He has spent the last twenty years working with Dean Rand on the *Discovery* as a naturalist while also photographing and exploring the Nellie Juan–College Fiord Wilderness Study Area (WSA). Hugh is a contributing photographer for *Arctic Wings: Birds of the Arctic National Wildlife Refuge* and *On Arctic Ground* (both published by Braided River). Hugh's hope is to see permanent wilderness designation for the WSA. To learn more about Hugh's photography and natural history interpretation work visit www.hughrosephotography.com.

ROBIN MILLER

TORI VANDERSOMMEN

BRAIDED RIVER®

BRAIDED RIVER, the conservation imprint of MOUNTAINEERS BOOKS, combines photography and writing to bring a fresh perspective to key environmental issues facing western North America's wildest places. Our books reach beyond the printed page as we take these distinctive voices and vision to a wider audience through lectures, exhibits, and multimedia events. Our goal is to build public support for wilderness preservation campaigns, and inspire public action. This work is made possible through the book sales and contributions made to Braided River, a 501(c)(3) nonprofit organization. Please visit BraidedRiver.org for more information on events, exhibits, speakers, and how to contribute to this work.

Braided River books may be purchased for corporate, educational, or other promotional sales. For special discounts and information, contact our sales department at 800.553.4453 or mbooks@mountaineersbooks.org.

THE MOUNTAINEERS, founded in 1906, is a nonprofit outdoor activity and conservation organization, whose mission is "to explore, study, preserve, and enjoy the natural beauty of the outdoors . . ." Mountaineers Books supports this mission by publishing travel and natural history guides, instructional texts, and works on conservation and history.

Send or call for our catalog of more than 800 outdoor titles:
Mountaineers Books
1001 SW Klickitat Way, Suite 201
Seattle, WA 98134
800.553.4453
www.mountaineersbooks.org

ISBN 978-1-68051-106-2

Manufactured in China on FSC®-certified paper, using soy-based ink.

MIX
Paper from
responsible sources
FSC® C008047

For more information, visit www.braidedriver.org

© 2018 by Debbie Miller

Publisher: Helen Cherullo
Project Manager: Janet Kimball
Developmental Editor: Ellen Wheat
Copyeditor: Chris Dodge
Cover and Book Designer: Kate Basart/Union Pageworks
All photographs by Hugh Rose unless otherwise noted.
Cartographer: Benchmark Maps
Scientific Advisor: Erin McKittrick

Origin of the Name on page 162 excerpted from *Chugach Legends* and reprinted by permission of the Chugach Alaska Corporation. All rights reserved.
Journal 58, May–June 1899, Harriman Expedition to Alaska, Part I, San Francisco to Harriman Fiord, Image 41, and *Journal 59, June–July 1899, Harriman Expedition to Alaska, Part II*, Image 4, reproduced with permission, John Muir Papers, Holt-Atherton Special Collections, University of the Pacific Library. © 1984 Muir-Hanna Trust.

FRONTISPIECE: *A sea otter mother and an older pup rest together on a small ice floe in Surprise Inlet near the face of the Surprise Glacier. Most pups are born in springtime, but sea otters can mate and pup any time of year. This pup was likely born in early winter the year before.* | PAGE 2: *An aerial view of Meares Glacier* | PAGE 4: *Mount Denson towers over a lone orca swimming northward into Prince William Sound near Hinchinbrook Entrance.* | PAGE 5: *A massive pillar of ice, equal in height to a fifteen-story building, calves from the face of Harvard Glacier in College Fiord.* | PAGE 6: *Pink salmon choke a freshwater stream at the head of Wells Bay during the annual August salmon run.* | PAGE 7: *A purse seiner hauls in a net full of pink salmon from the coastal waters near Esther Island. Four species of Pacific salmon spawn in the thousands of streams that feed into the Prince William Sound.* | PAGE 8: *Tufted puffins perch near the entrance to their burrow in the rainforest on Glacier Island.* | PAGE 9: *A dramatic sunset over the snow-covered Kenai Mountains near Eshamy Lagoon on the western side of Prince William Sound* | PAGE 10: *A black bear looks up from feeding on a pink salmon in McClure Bay.* | PAGE 11: *Moss-covered old-growth Sitka spruce trunk and branches, Glacier Island* | PAGE 12: *On a calm August evening, a harbor seal and pup rest on an ice floe, a safe birthplace created by a calving tidewater glacier.* | PAGE 13: *Ninety percent of the world's western sandpipers pass through the Copper River Delta every May.* | PAGE 14: *Harbor seals avoid predators, such as killer whales, by giving birth to their pups on ice floes near tidewater glaciers.* | PAGE 176: *Black bear, Chugach National Forest, Nellie Juan–College Fiord Wilderness Study Area*

Library of Congress Cataloging-in-Publication Data on file at https://lccn.loc.gov/2017042376